Being a Deacon Today

In 2005 Rosalind Brown was appointed Canon Residentiary at Durham Cathedral. Previously she was Vice Principal of the Ordained Local Ministry Scheme in the Diocese of Salisbury and a staff member of the Southern Theological Education and Training Scheme, based at Sarum College, Salisbury. Originally a town planner, she moved to the United States where she was a member of an Episcopal Religious Community and was ordained in the Episcopal Church. Rosalind is the author, with Christopher Cocksworth, of *Being a Priest Today* (Canterbury Press, 2002) and of several prize-winning hymn texts, some of which are published in *Sing! New Words for Worship* by Rosalind Brown, Jeremy Davies and Ron Green (Sarum College Press, 2004). She chaired the Diocese of Salisbury's Working Party which produced the report *The Distinctive Diaconate* (Sarum College Press, 2003).

Praise for *Being a Priest Today* by Rosalind Brown and Christopher Cocksworth

Here is a book . . . which may be an inspiration to ordinands and a help to priests in finding renewed focus and confidence in their calling.
Theology

A wise, comprehensive and deeply biblical book . . .
Epworth Review

Here is wisdom, knowledge and experience . . . a rich source of inspiration.
The Reader

Realistic, human and understanding, yet profoundly inspirational . . . a coherent and glowing book.
St Albans and Oxford Ministry Course

Being a Deacon Today

*Exploring a distinctive ministry
in the Church and in the world*

Rosalind Brown

morehouse

© 2005 Rosalind Brown

First published in Great Britain in 2005
by the Canterbury Press Norwich
(a publishing imprint of Hymns Ancient &
Modern Limited, a registered charity)
St Mary's Works, St Mary's Plain,
Norwich, Norfolk, NR3 3BH

www.scm-canterburypress.co.uk

Morehouse Publishing,
P.O. Box 1321, Harrisburg, PA 17105

Morehouse Publishing, The Tower Building,
11 York Road, London SE1 7NX

Morehouse Publishing is a Continuum imprint.

Library of Congress Cataloging-in-Publication Data

Brown, Rosalind.
   Being a deacon today : exploring a distinctive ministry
in the church and in the world / Rosalind Brown.
      p. cm.
   Includes bibliographical references.
   ISBN 0-8192-2201-1 (pbk.)
   1. Deacons.   2. Deacons—Anglican Communion.
   3. Anglican Communion—Clergy.   I. Title.
   BV680.B77 2005
   262'.143--dc22

                              2004030749

Typeset by Regent Typesetting, London
Printed and bound by
William Clowes

05 06 07 08 09 10   6 5 4 3 2 1

Contents

PART 3 THE GROUNDWORK OF DIACONAL MINISTRY

Foreword

In the Preface to the Ordinal in the Book of Common Prayer, it says: 'It is evident unto all men diligently reading Holy Scripture and ancient Authors, that from the Apostles' time there have been these Orders of Ministers in Christ's Church: Bishops, Priests, and Deacons.' While this has been the unbroken tradition from relatively early in the history of the Church, it has not always been self-evident. For many of the Reformers, a single order of ministers was sufficient, and as recently as 1974 a report of the Church of England[1] concluded that, as there was no functional task that belonged exclusively to deacons, the Church should consider abolishing the diaconate altogether. Did not deacons take away from, and indeed clericalize, ministry which properly belonged to lay people? Thinking like this lay behind many of the speeches – a number of them from Lay Readers – in the debate in the General Synod on the report *For Such a Time as This*,[2] the most recent in a series of reports on the diaconate in the Church of England.

But times have changed, and there is a renewed interest in the diaconate internationally as well as ecumenically. In their consideration of the nature of ministry, the churches are exploring the distinctive role of ministers, and have found substantial agreement.

The foundation of the Church's ministry is Christ. The Church ministers in his name, and all those who are baptized are called to use their gifts in ministering. From the whole company of the baptized, the Church calls, tests and forms some of its members in whom it recognizes distinctive gifts to be ordained to minister in Christ's name. By their ordination they are recognized as representative ministers, holding public office and excercising the Church's authority. Such ministers are not just appointed leaders, competent theologians and people of prayer who have a useful role in organizing the Church and keeping it in shape; ordained ministers point beyond themselves to Christ whose ministers they are, and reveal to the Church the key elements of his work and ministry. The ordained minister is not just a useful functionary: the minister is what Austin Farrer in a well-known sermon[3] described as 'a walking sacrament', a person who embodies the ministry of God in Christ that he or she represents.

Foundational to the ordained ministry is the incarnation: God in Christ comes among us and shares our life. He is the herald of God's Kingdom and proclaims its topsy-turvey nature by turning the normal human self-interested values upside down. But he does not simply talk about it; he does it. He values the poor and simple, sets a child up among his disciples, eats with tax gatherers and sinners and washes his disciples' feet like a household slave. If the first thing that God in Christ does is attend to his people and share their life in order that he may redeem and change it, then the deacon in his or her pastoral, liturgical and catechetical ministry is there to hold before the Church the truth that, before you can change people, you must attend to them and engage with them.

In this important and welcome study, Rosalind Brown, Vice Principal of the Salisbury Ordained Local Ministry Scheme, builds on the report for the diocese that she edited, *The Distinctive Diaconate*,[4] to produce a work of theological substance and practical importance for those who are seeking to explore diaconal ministry. That means not only those who are seeking to discern and 'hallow aright' the gifts that are being offered to the Church, whether in themselves or in others, but all those who are already deacons but are inclined to forget it – the priests and bishops of our Church.

For the diaconate – though a distinctive and wholly sufficient ministry in its own right – is the foundation of the ministry of all the ordained, and the Church's ministry as a whole would be the better if every priest and bishop remembered the pattern of Christ: that incarnation comes before redemption, and attentive engagement before change. In other words, listen before you speak; share people's lives before you try to impose your own ideas on them. God gives his Church a model of what to do in Christ, but not all his ministers have got this in their bones. Perhaps that is because we have for too long undervalued the diaconate, treating it as a probationary stepping stone to 'greater things' rather than valuing the diaconal ministry – ours included – as a foundational ministry in its own right.

If *Being a Deacon Today* helps the Church to understand and value the distinctive ministry of the deacon more, then the nature of the Church's ministry will change – and for the better.

David Stancliffe
Bishop of Salisbury

Acknowledgements

'Leaves and Flowers and Fruit' by Euros Bowen (1993) is reproduced with permission of Church in Wales Publications.

'The Word' and 'The Porch' by R. S. Thomas are published with permission of J. M. Dent, a division of Orion Publishing Group.

'Presence' and 'Ministers' by Padraig Daly are reproduced by permission of The Dedalus Press.

Extracts from *The Alternative Service Book 1980* and *Common Worship Ordinal Report by the Liturgical Commission 2004 (GS 1535)* are copyright © The Archbishops' Council and are reproduced by permission of Church House Publishing.

Thanks to those STETS students who have given permission for their stories to be included here anonymously.

Introduction

The Church of England's report *Mission Shaped Church*[1] was published while I was writing this book. It describes some of the new expressions of church that are emerging in response to challenging questions for the Church about its mission. The report identifies five values for missionary churches: they are focused on God the Trinity, incarnational, transformational, disciple-makers and relational.[2] All of these are at the heart of diaconal ministry and so if the Church is serious about mission, as it should be, then the Church should be serious about deacons. Deacons embody the Church in mission, encouraging and facilitating the ministry of all the baptized.

The Church of England has generally lost sight of the distinctive ministry of the deacon, seeing it as a rite of passage to priesthood, or, when women could not be ordained priest, as an ordained, non-presidential ministry open to women. Not only has this diminished the ministry of the deacon, it has also deprived the Church of a vital resource in ministry and mission. It is encouraging that across the world and across denominations, the ministry of the deacon is being recovered. Deacons stand at the threshold of the church and the world, not on their own but leading others in mission in the world and in worship in church. Essentially the ministry of the deacon is the ministry of the Church and at the heart of the diaconal vocation is a love that reflects the love of Christ. Deacons are lovers – lovers of God, lovers of God's Church, the body of Christ, and lovers of God's world. Diaconal ministry has three particular strands – enabling people to worship, providing pastoral care and proclaiming the gospel. Deacons are also role models and catalysts for the baptismal ministry of all Christians.

This book has various origins. In 2002 Christopher Cocksworth and I published *Being a Priest Today* and while writing it we found ourselves searching in the Christian tradition for the wisdom of the past on priestly ministry. I was aware as I did this that some of what I read was essentially about diaconal ministry, but that it was subsumed in priestly ministry, perhaps because the Church has lost a sense of what it means to be a deacon. At the same time I was asked to chair a working party for the Diocese of Salisbury on the ministry of deacons.[3] That gave me the opportunity to do more digging around in the tradition, this time with the diaconate in focus. The preparation of that report convinced me, if I had not been convinced before, of two things. First, that the Church needs to recognize the distinctive ministry of deacons and to affirm and support those for whom this is their vocation, seeing them not as apprentice priests but as ministers in their own right. Secondly, that for the majority who are ordained deacon and subsequently are ordained priest, the diaconate needs to be recovered from the false idea that it is just a time of transition before the 'real' priestly ministry begins. Instead, it should be welcomed as a time (perhaps more than a year) in which to live into diaconal ministry unencumbered by the additional responsibilities of priestly ministry that will eventually develop rather than supersede diaconal ministry.

The response to *Being a Priest Today* encouraged me to develop the work on the ministry of deacons into a similar exploration of what it means to be a deacon: not just for the gradually increasing numbers for whom the diaconate is a distinctive vocation, but also for the majority for whom diaconal ministry is now, or will be, expressed alongside and within priestly ministry. If this book reclaims 'the diaconal year' as simply the first of a lifetime of diaconal years then it has achieved its aim.

As with *Being a Priest Today*, I write as an Anglican but have drawn from the wider Christian tradition and hope that this is helpful to deacons in many denominations, even where our understandings of diaconal ministry differ.[4] I am grateful to the Deacons Group in the Diocese of Salisbury for their lived examples of what is written about here, to students I have known through my work in training people for ordination as I have shared their path towards ordination and diaconal ministry in the Church of England and the Methodist Church, and to colleagues and students in the United Reformed Church who have kept before us the work of Church Related Community Workers.

The shape of the book falls into three sections. The first arises from our work in Salisbury where we identified three locations for the ministry of the deacon: in the church, in the world and on the margins – these being both the margins of the world, and the margin or threshold between the church and the world, epitomized in the church doorstep over which the deacon leads people in both directions. Deacons are church people, also at home in the world, and liminal people who are comfortable living on boundaries. The former Archbishop of Canterbury, Robert Runcie, in his enthronement sermon in 1980, spoke of his essentially diaconal desire: 'I long to be able to speak, while Archbishop, with men and women who stand outside the Christian church. But I must stand also not at the edge but at the very centre of the Christian company as supporter and encourager.' In those sentences he catches the essential balance of diaconal ministry in the church and in the world. We belong in both church and world, and therefore on the margins of both.

The second section draws its themes from the Church of England's 2001 report, *For Such a Time as This*,[5] which identifies three strands to the ministry of the deacon: liturgical, pastoral and catechetical. Here the deacon is attendant, agent and bearer of a message. The more I have explored these themes, the more I have been amazed at the genius that insists that they be held together for the Church by the deacon: far from being unrelated or even opposed to each other, one without the other two is incomplete – worship loses touch with life, teaching becomes purely academic and not transformative, and pastoral care becomes secular social work. That is not to downplay the value of each in its own right. Many lay people are called to them in daily life and some are authorized by the Church to share in ministry in this way, but the deacon embodies their integration and in doing so reflects the ministry of Jesus Christ. Diaconal ministry is not just the caring, social work arm of the Church that some assume it to be; the deacon is a constant reminder to the Church of its sharing in Christ's servant ministry as the deacon encourages and helps all Christians to live into their baptismal vocation.

The third section of the book looks at some of the behind-the-scenes work in the life of the deacon if he or she is to fulfil this vocation. This reflects the bishop's reminder that '[t]o serve this royal priesthood, God has given a variety of ministries. Deacons are ordained that God's self-giving in Christ may be made visible and his people equipped to make known his love. Christ is the pattern of their calling and their commission; as he washed the feet of his disciples, so they must wash the feet of others.'[6] For this to happen there must be focus and growth in the deacon's own life. The titles of these chapters were originally faith, hope and love (I Corinthians 13), but I prefer the more active imperative of 'Pray', 'Love', 'Remember' that Shakespeare immortalized.[7] They are different ways of saying the same thing since prayer is the expression of faith, and memory bears fruit in hope.

This book keeps returning to the theological underpinning of the incarnation. That is inevitable in a book on diaconal ministry which draws its passion from the incarnate love of God in Jesus Christ. But that should not be interpreted as a downplaying of other theological truths, such as the redemptive work of God in Christ, or the history of God's engagement with the people in the period before the incarnation. It is a reflection of the fact that deacons are in one sense a prism through which the light of the incarnation shines, and a challenge to the Church to live in and engage with the world which God so loved, seeking and finding God's presence in all of life. Esther de Waal writes of 'unearth(ing) God in our midst',[8] which is a very diaconal and incarnational thing to do.

Every year I attend ordinations across the south of England and it is fascinating to reflect on how different the same liturgy can be. What is said is the same, what is done is the same in the sense that certain things have to happen. But each diocese puts its own spin on its understanding of diaconal ministry by the way it is all done. The theology is embodied and nuanced by the actions, and my experience at ordinations is always an object lesson that what we do often speaks louder than what we say. That is true in the life of each deacon, and so the words of this book are offered not as prescription or straitjacket, but as words to be interpreted and lived in the light of local circumstances. The diaconal vocation is always a blend of being and doing: '[To] define a deacon simply by "being" is inadequate; to define it simply by function runs the risk of reducing the church to one more human agency among others.'[9]

I am aware that I write as someone who is not at present engaged in the front line of diaconal ministry in a local church setting, and therefore have more to learn from others than they from me. But

I hope that the opportunity that my work gives me to explore the writings of the Christian tradition, to which I have deliberately given considerable emphasis in this book, and which is offered as part of my catechetical ministry among those on the journey towards ordination, is of help to those called to be deacons and will bear fruit in the life of all baptized Christians.

Rosalind Brown
Salisbury, Michaelmas 2004

PART I

THE LOCATION OF
DIACONAL MINISTRY

I

The Deacon in the Church

Loving the church

Deacons are rooted in the local church, living out with the people there – whether regular worshippers or not – a life that reflects the love of Christ. In the Church of England there can be no ordination without a title parish in which to serve, because there can be no deacon without a community to love and serve, and with whom to worship God. Deacons speak and act in the church's name whether in the public eye or in private, so that '[a] lonely deacon saying his [sic] Office in an empty church speaks in the name of the Church no less than the bishop pontificating in his cathedral'.[1]

This presupposes that the deacon has a history in the church, a history of being known by the people, of worshipping and praying, of serving and celebrating, of laughing and crying, of studying and relaxing. In the nineteenth-century novel *The Little Minister*, James Barrie puts these words into the mouth of a retiring minister speaking to his very young successor: 'You must join the family, Mr Dishart, or you are only a minister once a week.'[2] In this instance the words are spoken to a minister moving into a church and they remain true for those deacons who move into a new church upon ordination, but they are a prerequisite of those deacons whose vocation is identified and lived within a church where they are known, tested by the unglamorous routine of daily life lived locally. Being a deacon requires joining the family; it is incarnational. And, as we all know, families can be a source both of joy and irritation. We may love them easily, or we may have to work at it, but love them we must if our ministry is to be Christ-like and not a source of stumbling – congregations have an uncanny knack of knowing if they are loved or merely tolerated. Perhaps the temptation to the latter is greater for those deacons who know that in due course they will move on elsewhere.

Ronnie Aitchison, a Methodist Deacon, writes perceptively:

Ministry must be offered to the body before the body can offer its ministry to the community. . . . In I John 4.19 it says, 'we love, because he first loved us'. A congregation that does not feel loved will find it difficult to offer love. A deacon, called to represent Christ who serves, has a clear responsibility to enable the congregation to feel loved so that he or she can enable them to love.[3]

However, realism is essential and Eugene Peterson, an American Presbyterian pastor, dispossesses us of any false sense of idealization of the Church when he writes of its local manifestation:

St Paul talked about the foolishness of preaching; I would like to carry on about the foolishness of the congregation. Of all the ways in which to engage in the enterprise of church, this has to be the most absurd – this haphazard collection of people who somehow get assembled into pews on Sundays, half-heartedly sing a few songs most of them don't like, tune in and out of a sermon according to the state of their digestion and the preacher's decibels, awkward in their commitments and jerky in their prayers.

But the people in these pews are also people who suffer deeply and find God in their suffering. These are men and women who make love commitments, are faithful to them through trial and temptation, and bear fruits of righteousness, spirit-fruits that bless the people around them. . . .

The congregation is topsoil – seething with energy and organisms that have incredible capacities for assimilating death and participating in resurrection. The only biblical stance is awe. When we see what is before us, really before us, pastors take off their shoes before the *shekinah* of congregation.[4]

It is this wonderful ragbag of saints that deacons love and serve, and whom they lead in their own love and service. To be a deacon is to share in ministry flowing from the diaconal ministry of Jesus Christ. It is to be caught up in ministry that is incarnational, rooted in place, in time, in life. And it is the privilege of the deacon to be a catalyst for the ministry of all the baptized, encouraging and freeing them by our example to live for the glory of God. The words of Nelson Mandela, not originally about deacons, nevertheless express diaconal ministry that liberates and stirs the church into action:

> You are a child of God . . .
> We were born to make manifest
> The glory of God that is within us.
> It's not just in some of us,
> It's within everyone.
> As we let our lights shine
> We unconsciously give other people
> Permission to do the same.
> As we are liberated from our own fear
> Our presence automatically liberates others.[5]

Love for the church is integral to our love for God. Thus, writing of the teaching and example of Archbishop Michael Ramsey, Douglas Dales observes:

> How Christians relate to the church is part of their relationship with Christ, it is not additional to it. 'Its oneness, in which they share, speaks the truth about him.' It follows then that the more deeply they enter into the reality of the church's life in Christ, the more committed they will become to its essential unity as their consciousness of its mystery grows.[6]

Without this integration of love for God's church with our love for God, we are in danger of either setting our passion for the church above our love for God or acting independently of the church which is the body of Christ. The danger of the first is that we draw people to the church as institution rather than draw people to God, or become pedantic idealists of an institution. The danger of the second is that we draw people to ourselves as God's minister, rather than into the fellowship of the church. Tragically, history bears witness to the damage caused by people who have fallen into these traps. If we do not learn as deacons to love and serve God and the church, all our subsequent ministry will be open to these dangers.

Theologically, what is at stake here is the Trinitarian source of all the Church's life and ministry. At the heart of Trinitarian theology is dynamic mystery. The theological concept of *perichoresis* points to the interpenetration of one Person of the Trinity in another, coinherence without confusion. The actions of each Person are always co-operative, there is a hinterland to the actions of each Person. Thus whilst each may act in a distinctive way, this is never divorced from the other two Persons who are involved in the action of the other and in the dance of the Trinity (the root of *perichoreuo* is 'to dance around'). Since in Christ – who was fully human and fully divine – we are caught up in the life and ministry of the Trinity, we are invited to 'join the dance', be drawn into the mystery. And thus love for God embraces love of God's Church, the body of Christ. This is all embodied in the Eucharist when the church gathers to share the Trinitarian life of God. There is no diaconal ministry without service in the Eucharist when the deacon, with others, enables the church to express its identity as God's people. And at the end of the Eucharist when the deacon sends out the worshippers ('the topsoil seething with energy') to 'Go in peace to love and serve the Lord' the deacon articulates and embodies the truth of God's love, and thus our love, not just for the church but the world. The Eucharist leads us straight into each other's lives, lives that Christ shares.

Ministry with others

Because God is Trinity, diaconal ministry – which reflects that of Christ – is always collaborative, and the relationship of the deacon to all the other members of the church is a litmus test of that person's diaconal ministry. Deacons do not take over and do it all. That can be hard to accept in a world where so often a person is valued for what they do and where those who are newly ordained feel a pressure to be seen to prove their ability, as well as a need to express their enthusiasm. We need to remember that deacons point to the truth that who we are, rather than what we do, is the basis of life in the church. There can be a temptation to take over the work of others and thus disempower them, but equally the church can collude with the deacon, letting him or her do the work of ministry in order that others may be excused. Instead of these scenarios, the deacon is called to focus in a particular way the ministry of the church and enable others to recognize and develop their own gifts and skills so that together the church expresses its ministry as the diaconal body of Christ. In an address to the North American Association of Deacons, the Rt Revd Tom Ray described deacons as people who reveal and shine a light on the servant ministry that is already embedded in all our lives, often unheralded and unappreciated. The diaconate is a clear window through which to see a dimension and depth of meaning of our own baptism. Deacons are not set apart by ordination into special territory, but in order to reveal to Christians the serving ministry that has always hallowed our homes, workplaces, community and church. He describes the deacon as exploding our awareness and understanding of diaconal ministry into a daily ministry; having ordained deacons makes an invisible ministry visible and recognized as part of Christ's ministry.[7] Therefore there can be no sense that the deacon's ministry is 'better' or more valid than that of people who are not ordained, because the deacon serves alongside others in the church in mutual collaboration, support and encouragement.

When considering the ministry of the deacon in relation to other ministries, in the Diocese of Salisbury we developed the rainbow image as another way of exploring the mystery of ministry that is born of the Trinitarian *perichoresis*. Whilst lacking the dynamism of the dance imagery, looking at a rainbow illustrates that if we try to demarcate the boundary where, for example, red meets orange, we will never find it. There is a focus to the colour that is revealed in the depth of the colour at its heart, but the colour is not lost when that depth is lost and it begins to merge with another colour. But if we look at the rainbow in its total beauty, we can see red and we can see orange, and they cannot exist without each other and still belong to the rainbow. Another way of looking at this is to consider a photographer taking pictures of flowers. The focus could be on one flower in perfect focus: its delicate beauty is seen in great clarity but the rest of the flowers are out of focus. Alternatively, there can be a photograph in which all flowers are in focus but the details are lost. The analogy with collaborative ministry should be clear – if we begin from the Anglican view of the threefold order of ordained ministry and the importance of lay ministry, then we have the rainbow or the bed of flowers. Or we can examine each ministry in detail, accepting that the others will go out of focus or the precise boundary will never be found. Neither way is better than the other, and there is no value judgement that declares yellow better than red in a rainbow or a rose better than a violet in a garden.[8]

In the Church of England, where Reader ministry is well established and valued, there is a danger of misunderstanding the ministry of a deacon as duplicating, even replacing, that of a Reader. Nothing could be further from the truth. Readers were established in the nineteenth century as a lay ministry of teaching, preaching and liturgical leadership, a ministry that has its origins in the earlier minor order of lector. This is quite different in origin and focus from the ministry of the deacon. Both are called by their baptism to a common witness in the world, but in addition to this the focused ministry of Readers, who are lay people, is largely in the church during worship where they lead worship, preach and teach, whilst that of deacons, who are ordained, is largely outside the church doors in the world. There may be some overlap of ministry with Readers, most obviously with deacons who expect to be ordained priest in due course and thus will be entrusted with a preaching and teaching ministry themselves, but this can be seen as an expression of the perichoretic dance of the Trinity, in which we are caught up and at times find ourselves with our various callings dancing the same steps together for a while, before continuing the dance in different ways.

From the earliest decades of the Church there has been a particular relationship between the bishop and the deacons who assisted with administration for the bishop and dispersed the Church's charities. This lies behind the ministry of archdeacons who still deal with many day-to-day matters in the diocese on behalf of the bishop. It is too simplistic merely to read back into the early Church what we find today, but we can note the sense of the deacons as enablers of the ministry of the bishop and the Church. Antonia Lynn[9] uses the image of the deacon as the 'old retainer' servant who knows the family he or she has served for years, and uses that knowledge to take the initiative and keep it running smoothly. To do this, the deacon need not be a priest but should have theological training and an immersion in the Church that enables him or her to understand its needs and its ways. The deacon should be content to be behind the scenes, facilitating the public ministry of the bishop. Care and attention to detail are paramount, along with unflappability and an ability in administration.

Not all deacons will work that closely with a bishop, although there are recent examples of deacons serving as Bishop's deacon.[10] In the Anglican Church normally all deacons work with priests and it is not really possible for there to be a deacon without a priest, even though there are examples of deacons who have served as Deacon in Charge of a parish, particularly when women in the Church of England were ordained deacon but not priest. This is not ideal and my experience as Deacon in Charge of a church in the United States was that the responsibilities of oversight prevented me from living into diaconal ministry in its own right. Ronnie Aitchison describes the situation in his local Methodist Church when the absence of a presbyter led to pressure from the congregation for him, a deacon, to be licensed under deprivation measures to fulfil some presbyteral ministry. In the Methodist Church, the deacon's ministry is quite distinct from that of the presbyter, since there is direct rather than sequential ordination.[11] He writes:

> The use of deacons as substitutes for presbyters does a disservice in two ways. First it devalues the diaconal role, with the laity struggling to understand the difference in the two roles . . . second, it creates a point of stress in the deacons' own ministry as they still desire to fulfil their diaconal calling and to demonstrate and encourage *diakonia*. Where the deacon is called upon to undertake the presbyter's role and function it is the representation of Christ at the table which comes to be seen as the most important ministerial role. Representing the foot-washing Christ becomes difficult because of limitations of time and because the congregation, presented with a familiar and comfortable image, will be reluctant to accept a different perspective on ministry.[12]

Aitchison makes an important point here: if the deacon is distracted from representing Christ the foot-washer – the calling of all Christians, not just the ordained – the congregation loses the model for its own discipleship. Once the deacon is seen presiding at table the congregation can let itself off the hook and fail to follow the deacon's example of service. That shifts the emphasis away from the servant ministry of the whole church which the deacon embodies. This highlights the emphasis from Bishop Tom Ray of the deacon's ministry as shining a light on the ministry of service that we all

share, and the difficulty of doing this when the emphasis is entirely
on the presbyteral ministry at table. In the Anglican Church the
deacon has an important and visible role in the eucharistic liturgy
which complements that of the priest and placards in the liturgy the
essential diaconal element of all ministry. Deacons work collaboratively, offering with confidence and not apology a non-presidential,
representative ministry that makes visible and represents Christ's
own diaconal ministry. Deacons need to develop leadership gifts,
for they are indeed leaders, but gifts that reflect a willingness to be
collaborative leaders. At an ecumenical consultation on ordination
one speaker observed that misunderstanding of *diakonia* as servanthood has led to a refusal to lead.[13] There is an art in leadership that
enables others to fulfil their own responsibilities without unsettling
or unseating them. To be among people, as Jesus was, as one who
serves[14] demands distinctive leadership and organizational gifts
which equip and free others to do their work well. There is a creative dynamic between servanthood that leads well and servanthood
that is comfortable behind the scenes.

The Rule of Benedict gives us some insights which, although
initially for monastics, are helpful in exploring diaconal ministry
in the church. According to Benedict, the abbot or abbess leads
the community by pointing out all that is good and holy, 'more by
example than by words, proposing God's commandments to a recep-
tive community with words, but demonstrating God's instructions
to the stubborn and dull by a living example'.[15] Perhaps Benedict
could be blunter in his language about his monastics than we can be
about our congregations, but his insight that the 'stubborn and dull'
need teaching by example is an insight for diaconal ministry. A little
later in the same chapter Benedict expands further on the approach
that the abbess and abbot need when directing souls and serving
people with different temperaments. They should variously coax,
reprove and encourage, and to do this they must accommodate and
adapt themselves to each person's character and intelligence. One
size does not fit all in such ministry, and yet there is never any sense
that Benedict compromises his aims or standards, he just adjusts his
way of getting there. Deacons can learn from this example.

Later in his Rule, Benedict turns to the qualifications of the
Monastery Cellarer, who handled the monastery supplies and
was therefore the recipient of many cases of special pleading and

unreasonable demands, as well as the routine emergency needs when an unexpected guest showed up. Deacons may recognize the scenario! What does Benedict look for in the cellarer? What might we look for in a deacon? It is not just administrative excellence, although no doubt that counts, but he wants someone who is 'wise, mature in conduct, temperate, not an excessive eater, not proud, excitable, offensive, dilatory, or wasteful, but God-fearing, and like a parent to the whole community'.[16] He or she should take care of everything under the orders of the prioress or abbot. When confronted with an unreasonable demand, the cellarer should find a way to reject the improper request without rejecting with disdain the person who causes distress. It is summed up in Benedict's words, 'The cellarer should not annoy the members.' Those who have lived in close-knit communities know how easy it is to be annoyed by someone else, but we are to resist the temptation to cause that annoyance deliberately. Monastics are very realistic people and another early monastic, Evagrius Ponticus, recognized that, although this is not always easy, it is possible: 'It is not possible to love all the brethren to the same degree. But it is possible to associate in a manner that is free of resentment and hatred.'[17] Deacons, like cellarers, are to be peaceable and peace-makers in the way they handle the distribution of supplies to those who need them – whether that is emergency food supplies or the Sunday School crayons. In fact, Benedict draws a parallel between the material utensils with which the cellarer is concerned and the sacred vessels of the altar, and insists that they should be treated with the same care. This attitude to people and material things is at the heart of the ministry of the deacon and oils the wheels for the life of all in the church.

Being a representative person

The Church is charged with going into all the world to preach the gospel and so diaconal ministry is not just ministry in the Church but the ministry of the Church in the world. Deacons must therefore be people whom the Church can trust and wants as its representatives (hence the congregation's affirmation that it is their will that the deacon be ordained). They must also be people who are comfortable in the public eye. At ordination, the Church calls deacons to share in the ministry entrusted to the Church and to be its representatives. Thus the bishop says this to those to be ordained:

> Deacons are called to work with the bishop and the priests with whom they serve as heralds of Christ's kingdom. They are to proclaim the gospel in word and deed, as agents of God's purposes of love. They are to serve the community in which they are set, bringing to the Church the needs and hopes of all the people. They are to work with their fellow members in searching out the poor and weak, the sick and lonely, and those who are oppressed and powerless, reaching into the forgotten corners of the world, that the love of God may be made visible. . . .
>
> Deacons are to seek nourishment from the Scriptures; they are to study them with God's people, that the whole church may be equipped to live out the gospel in the world. They are to be faithful in prayer, expectant and watchful for the signs of God's presence, as he reveals his kingdom among us.
>
> We trust that you are fully determined, by the grace of God, to give yourself wholly to his service, that you may draw all his people into that new life which God has prepared for those who love him.[18]

The wording of this declaration draws, theologically, on biblical research that was not available at the time when the 1550 Ordinal, which was bound into the 1662 Book of Common Prayer, was drafted. That Ordinal reflected an understanding of diaconal ministry as essentially assistance to the priest in divine service and – mainly in the absence of the priest – baptism and preaching. It also included identifying the needy in the parish so that the priest could ensure those in need received the alms from parishioners. By the time of the *Alternative Service Book (1980)* the ministry of the deacon was described in this way:

> A deacon is called to serve the Church of God and to work with its members in caring for the poor, the needy, the sick and all who are in trouble. He [*sic*] is to strengthen the faithful, search out the careless and indifferent and to preach the word of God in the place to which he is licensed. A deacon assists the priest under whom he serves, in leading the worship of the people, especially in the administration of the Holy Communion. He may baptise

when required to do so. It is his general duty to do such pastoral work as is entrusted to him.[19]

This emphasizes the servant role of the deacon, working as assistant rather than in collaborative ministry with the priest. It sounds more like a training contract for a newly ordained deacon anticipating ordination to the priesthood, rather than an experienced deacon with a well-developed ministry. Although it has abandoned the 1550 language of the diaconate as an 'inferior ministry' there is still a hierarchical feel to it.

Recent research, primarily by John Collins,[20] draws out a wider understanding of the ministry of a deacon in the early centuries by looking at the meaning of the word in secular Greek usage. This leads Collins to criticize as inadequate the modern narrow definition of *diakonia* as charitable works. He argues that in some sectors of the Church, notably those influenced by the teaching of Calvin, Acts 6 has been used to make social work the defining work of deacons.[21] He criticizes this on the basis that Luke chooses not to use the word 'deacon' even though he was familiar with all that the *diakon-* words stood for in Greek language, religion and culture. Instead, Collins argues that throughout Acts Luke uses the *diakon-* words for the ministry by which the Word of God spread from Jerusalem, initially by the first disciples and then by Paul. He concludes that the ancient audience of Acts would understand Acts 6.1 to mean that the Greek-speaking widows were being overlooked in the daily preaching of the Word and, since the Twelve could not leave the public proclamation in the temple, these women needed preachers who could speak to them in Greek, preferably at home when they came together at their tables.

Collins suggests that the emphasis of service is not the menial service of others but service of God expressed in fulfilling the ministry to which one is called. This contrasts greatly with the Reformation emphasis (expressed, for example, in the Lutheran Church's understanding of deacons) on service as essentially social work. Collins writes of the deacon as spokesperson, envoy, courier, go-between entrusted with important tidings; as ambassador, mediator, person commissioned to carry out a task and act on behalf of a person in authority; and as attendant within a household, on whose behalf the deacon performs various tasks which are not limited to waiting at table. These can be summarized under the three headings of the deacon as bearer of a message, as agent and as attendant. All carry connotations of responsible agency on behalf of a person in authority, and commitment to fulfil a vital task. Collins discounts any implications of inferiority or menial service. In the second century Ignatius bore out this representative emphasis, writing that the deacons must be shown respect since they represent Jesus Christ, just as the bishop represents the Father and the presbyters are like God's council.[22]

Collins's work is receiving a mixed reception in the Church. Nevertheless, he is forcing the Church to reconsider its inherited understanding of the ministry of the deacon, casting it in much wider terms than assistance to the priest and service of people in need. In a different study Deidre Good[23] frees the word 'meek' from the distorting connotation of servility, reclaiming instead its classical meaning which is expressed in the case of kingship that is meek as the opposite of tyrannical or despotic. This too has implications for our understanding of the ministry of Christ and of the Church's diaconal ministry.

For Such a Time as This, the Church of England's 2001 report on the ministry of deacons, develops these lines of thinking. The deacon is invested with authority by Christ, through the Church in the person of the bishop. The deacon is not set apart for menial service nor is expected to exhibit more humility than others, or to bear more than a fair share of suffering for Christ's sake. Instead the deacon is a person on a mission, an ambassador or messenger, making connections, building bridges, faithfully delivering a mandate. The deacon is the visible sign of what the Church is called to be, representing to the Church and to the world its authoritative calling as the servant of God and God's people. The deacon, in common with all the ordained, is to promote, release and clarify the nature of the Church. Through ordination the Church sets the deacon apart to be a public, representative person whom it sends as herald and ambassador of the Kingdom. The deacon must be a person in whom the Church can place its trust. This setting apart and recognition of responsibility entrusted plays out in many ways in the life of the deacon who is no longer his or her own person, but the Church's person: ultimately Christ's own through baptism but now also the Church's public face through ordination.[24]

Earlier, in 1988, the Church of England had written of the two-way representative ministry of the deacon, '[T]he ordained deacon represents in a special way the diaconal nature of God in Christ to the Church, and through the church, to the wider community.'[25] This brings with it enormous responsibilities and a vocation to holiness of life. This is shared with all Christians and thus, just over four hundred years ago, Richard Hooker wrote of religious duty that is expressed both as individuals and as members of the body of Christ. In the ethos of his day the latter was more significant than the former, an understanding that comes hard to our individualistic culture:

> The holy and religious duty of service towards God concerneth us one way in that we are men, and another way in that we are joined as parts to that visible mystical body which is his Church. As men, we are at our own choice, both for time, and place, and form, according to the exigence of our own occasions in private; but the service, which we do as members of a public body, is public, and for that cause must needs be accounted so much worthier than the other, as a whole society of such condition exceedeth the worth of any one.[26]

The same basic thought is expressed in a different way by Sean Connolly, a Roman Catholic priest writing in the twenty-first century:

> There is no option to freelance here. When God calls us – whatever our vocation – he calls us to some definite service within the Church. When we live out our divine calling, we do so as a service to the Church and not purely for our own edification. The call to holiness – whether we mean 'common' or 'specific' – is never entirely a private and personal matter; it is always caught up with the very definition of *ecclesia*, for the Church itself is called to be one, holy, catholic and apostolic. In our vocation to holiness we are called to unity, not individualism, we are called through the apostolic community, not simply directly; we are called to serve generously the universal Church, and not merely those sections or traditions with which we have most in common. Looking at the scriptures, it is clear that the call to holiness is not about isolated dedication to the Lord.[27]

Vocation is both an individual and a corporate thing and has lifelong consequences which few fully grasp at the time of ordination; thus, in words written when only men were ordained in the Anglican Church:

> The term 'vocation' is frequently used as if it were simply a synonym for the ideas and desires in a man's own mind and heart: the fact that a real vocation involves being *called* – not choosing but being chosen – is widely ignored. . . . But where the vocation exists, a man has still to discover the demands that it makes upon him in the way of personal self-discipline, self-surrender, penitence and perseverance.[28]

Since, by our baptism, we are made members of the body of Christ, we are church people. In ordination, the Church lays special responsibilities on those called to diaconal ministry and, in calling them to be public representative persons, calls them also to greater attention to the detail of holy living. This makes demands on us and is not attention to detail for its own sake, but in order that the deacon has the resources for the ministry to which he or she is called. It is simply not possible to fulfil the ministry of a deacon and to live sloppily, hence the public examination by the bishop of those about to be ordained. These are not questions about the deacon's learning or skills – they have been inquired into already – but about the deacon's intentions with regard to his or her way of living as related to the Holy Scriptures, the doctrine of the Christian faith and the discipline of the Church. The Church wants to know about our intention to be diligent in prayer, reading scripture, and studying to deepen faith; to live according to the way of Christ; to promote peace, unity and love among Christian people; and to stir up the gift of God and make Christ known to all. The Church has the right to ask these questions and to hear the answers, because the deacon is to be its representative. Once the Church has heard the answers the people are themselves asked if it is their will that the person be ordained deacon. The people undertake to uphold and pray for the deacons in their ministry, thus establishing a reciprocity of responsibility and care from the start. And with this, there is also the promise of the continual empowering of the Spirit, as Richard Hooker expressed four hundred years ago:

> [W]e may most assuredly persuade ourselves that the hand which imposeth upon us the function of our ministry doth under the

same form of words so tie itself thereunto, that he which receiveth the burden is thereby forever warranted to have the Spirit with him and in him for his assistance, aid, countenance and support in whatsoever he faithfully doth to discharge his duty. Know . . . therefore that when we take Ordination we also receive the presence of the holy Ghost, partly to guide, direct and strengthen us in all our ways, and partly to assume unto itself for the more authority those actions which appertain to our place and calling . . .[29]

Once the deacon has been called, commissioned and ordained by the church, it is the deacon's vocation to enable the church to be itself in following Christ who gave his life for others. Therefore, baptism preparation is a significant part of diaconal ministry, helping people to recognize their own vocation to be disciples; and – once people are baptized – diaconal ministry is about stirring up Christians so that the church is radically faithful in its worship and its witness, recognizing both the personal and societal implications of being called into the diaconal ministry of the body of Christ. This is expressed by Philip Sheldrake, who writes:

> The Christian community in its vocation of catholicity does not merely engage in a mission of pouring itself out for the world as a prolongation of the kenosis of Jesus Christ. Rather the church *is*, most substantially, in its vocation of kenotic outpouring, in a transgression of its own boundaries, in overflowing excess, in leaving itself behind, in breaking itself open.[30]

The deacon, whose ministry is in the church, is charged with ministry that transgresses its boundaries, that steps across the threshold of the church and breaks itself open in the world which God so loves. To that context for ministry we turn next.

2

The Deacon in the World

Incarnation and ministry

If the deacon is to be a church person, at home in and loving the church, then the deacon must also be a very worldly person. Henry Scott Holland once observed: 'The more you believe in the Incarnation, the more you care about drains.'[1] The world in all its beauty and splendour, its tawdriness and despoliation, is God's and the locale for the Church's mission. The early Church's response to the Gnostic heresy gives the lie to any attempts to retreat into an other-worldly, non-material faith. Without rootedness in the world, life and ministry are meaningless. From the very beginnings of the biblical narrative, the story is of God who comes among us – asking the hiding Adam and Eve, 'Where are you?' (Genesis 3.9), saying, 'I have seen the misery of my people and have come down' (Exodus 3.7–8), and giving the name 'Emmanuel', 'God is with us', to the incarnate Son (Matthew 1.23). And it is this incarnational self-giving of God that sets our agenda as the people of God. In an uncomfortable challenge to the Anglo-Catholic Congress of 1923, Bishop Frank Weston said:

> You cannot claim to worship Jesus in the tabernacle if you do not pity Jesus in the slum. It is folly – it is madness – to suppose that you can worship Jesus in the sacraments and Jesus on the throne of glory when you are sweating Him in the bodies and souls of his children. You have your Mass, you have your altars . . . now go out into the highways and hedges and look for Jesus in the ragged and the naked, in the oppressed and the sweated, in those who have lost hope, and in those who are struggling to make good. Look for Jesus in them and when you have found Him, gird

yourself with His towel of fellowship and wash His feet in the person of his brethren.[2]

Kathleen Norris, writing of a small and isolated Presbyterian church in North Dakota, quotes a pastor speaking of this church, 'The thing that makes Hope [Church] so vibrant is that the congregation is so alive to the world.'[3] Engagement with our world gives zest and purpose to our ministry as we live out the incarnation. Therefore we must know our world. George Herbert recognized his need to know about tillage and pastorage if he was to be an effective minister to his people, on the basis that people are led to understand what they do not know by the route of what they do know.[4]

It is not uncommon to hear it said of a person who is about to be ordained, 'I hear you are going into the Church', to which two replies might be given: either, 'No more than when I was baptized', or, 'Yes, but only in order to come straight back out again.' Jesus was no recluse: we find him at weddings and dinner parties, debating with the leaders of the day, meeting all sorts of people from outcasts to the highly respectable, and clearly revelling in the beauty of nature. The picture is one of deep engagement with the world of Roman rulers, Jewish freedom fighters, taxes and illnesses, building collapses and rebellions. And it was the same for the early Church which was born in a politically unstable world and soon engaged with many cultures beyond Palestine. The world is God's, and Jesus prayed that his followers would not be taken out of it but would be protected from evil in it (John 17.14–19).

This is not an uncritical engagement with the world. The Old Testament prophets model an engagement that was objective and discerning, not afraid to speak out when the time came, politically astute and pastorally compassionate. Diaconal ministry takes its lead from this: deacons have a prophetic ministry in the world where injustice exists, and a pastoral ministry to people in need. Because they do this as the church's representative people there is a two-way movement – deacons lead the church into the world in mission, and the world into the church for prayer and action. Diaconal ministry has this world as its context, and deacons need to be happy there, able to see Christ in the midst of its life. It is reasonable for the church to expect in deacons evidence of engagement with the local community and awareness of what is happening in the wider world, along with the capacity to be a public representative person for the church, competent and comfortable in the public eye and respected by people beyond the church. In other words, deacons need to have a genuinely world-oriented and world-affirming perspective.

Alasdair Macintyre was not writing of diaconal ministry when he wrote lines that have import for deacons, charged as they are with engagement with the church and the world:

[T]he task of religion is to help see the secular as the sacred, the world as under God. When the sacred and the secular are separated, then ritual becomes the end not to the hallowing of the world, but in itself. Likewise if our religion is fundamentally irrelevant to our politics, then we are recognising the political as a realm outside the reign of God. To divide the sacred from the secular is to recognise God's action only within the narrowest limits.[5]

Rowan Williams took this one theological step further in his sermon at his enthronement in Canterbury Cathedral when he referred not just to sacred and secular, but to God's image in human beings.

The Christian will engage with passion in the world of our society and politics out of a real hunger and thirst to see God's image, the destiny of human beings to become God's sons and daughters come to light – and, it must be said, out of a real grief and fear of what the human future will be if this does not come to light. The church has to warn and to lament as well as to comfort.[6]

Deacons keep before the church the truth that all humans, not just Christians, are made in the image of God. There is vital wisdom in the deacon's embrace of responsibilities for action in the world and worship in church; this inbuilds the possibility for holistic ministry reflecting that of Christ. I am reminded of this every time I attend the morning Eucharist in Salisbury Cathedral and watch the early sun shine through the Prisoners of Conscience Window with its interpretation of the suffering of such prisoners in the light of the death of Jesus Christ, shown here as a prisoner of conscience. Above it all – the crucified Christ and our eucharistic celebration – shines the gold of God's glory, and from the cross a triangle of light falls on those who suffer and die for the sake of conscience. And next to the altar stands the Amnesty candle, surrounded by barbs, which bring the injustice of the world into the heart of our worship.

The model is the incarnation, culminating in the ascension when Jesus, fully human and bearing his scars, was taken into heaven. There is now a place in heaven for our scars and wounds and the deacon holds this truth before the Church and the world. The world can create institutions for dealing with some of the injustices of the world and the Church should be deeply engaged with them, but those institutions cannot deal with the alienation of the world from God: that is the Church's distinctive ministry. The Truth and Reconciliation Commission in South Africa is probably the best-known example of an institution that has made inroads into the dreadful legacies of alienation and injustice. The world should be able to expect to find small-scale examples of this same work for reconciliation in local churches, with deacons involved as agents of reconciliation – God's ambassadors appealing to people to be reconciled to God and to one another, thus embodying Paul's exhortations in 2 Corinthians 5.20. In Philippians 4.1–2 the church is commanded to help two women who have fallen out with each other, but we rush past these verses and miss their import: in the middle of a letter about profound theological matters, Paul drops in a command to deal with a spat between two women. Theology is lived out in the ups and downs of life, and if the church cannot deal with need among its members, how can we deal with the needs of the world?

John Donne compressed all this sense of responsibility for one another into his phrase 'no man is an island',[7] and Archbishop Robert Runcie expanded this when outlining reasons for the Church intervening in political matters. The occasion was a speech on 'Church and State' in 1984 and his message is summarized:

> First, there was the need to unpack the moral principles relating to any issue. Secondly, Christians must speak up for the poor and the powerless, both in body and spirit. His third principle was designed to be a reminder that no country is an island in more than the strictly geographical sense: that 'belonging' these days has an inescapable global perspective. The fourth principle he described as particularly Anglican. It was the responsibility to resist the mindless cults of unreason, both in religion and political life, and to strive for loyalty to truth.[8]

Runcie raises some challenging issues for the Church. Deacons need to be able to unpack moral principles for their congregations and to set an example in speaking for the poor and powerless. Using their minds in their catechetical and pastoral service, active in their local area, able to see beyond its boundaries so that no parish becomes totally parochial in its outlook, deacons are to be rooted and grounded in God's ways and God's word. The liberation theologians face the Church with the challenge of being caught up in God's love which meets people where they are, not necessarily where we'd like them to be. Thus Gustavo Gutiérrez, one of Peru's prophetic voices, writes: 'A true and full encounter with our neighbour requires that we experience the gratuitousness of God's love. Once we have experienced it our approach to others is purified of any tendency to impose an alien will on them. It is disinterested and respectful of their personalities, needs and aspirations.'[9]

There is a fine balance between this acceptance of others that respects them as people, and buying wholesale into the systems they and we inhabit, particularly where these are unjust, but also where they are enervating or mediocre, diminishing people who are created in the image of God. Ministry in the world should reflect Jesus' ministry that all might have life in all its fullness. Along with this we can never forget that the Church is called to holiness, to a way of life substantively different from that of the world. Kenneth Leech, writing out of years of experience of ministry in the East End of London, questions the tendency to separate morality from holiness, arguing that without holiness and a rigorous encounter with our own sins we will harden into a harsh, judgemental, moral posture. In the light of this, he calls for a recovery of holiness among Christians and – although he does not specifically articulate it – to a role for deacons in modelling this holiness. His last sentence points to the essential integration of diaconal pastoral and liturgical ministry.

Holiness was originally about separation, and this separatist emphasis should not be entirely abandoned. I believe that many Christians, particularly in what are misleadingly called 'mainstream' or 'liberal' churches, have tended to operate on a minimal basis of ethics: low expectation combined with high tolerance and compassion. While I am entirely in favour of compassion and of supporting people in their struggles and trials in a spirit of gentleness and understanding, there is an element in the gospel which speaks with a different voice, issues a different call, and articulates a different hunger. This is the voice of holiness, the call to heroic discipleship, the hunger for God. Separation from 'the world' – in the sense of the sinful and unjust demands and structures of the fallen world-order – remains a requirement for us if we are to follow the call to be transformed, not conformed.

Yet the specific thrust of the Christian sacramental tradition is to bring together the holy and the common. 'Holy Communion' is not only the name of the central Christian act of worship, it also sums up the whole meaning of Christian life, which is the practice of the holy in the midst of the common life of humankind.[10]

The local world

All this is fine in the abstract, but it takes shape and bears fruit in daily life. William Law wrote in his eighteenth-century call to a devout and holy life, 'If we are to be in Christ new creatures, we must show that we are so, by having new ways of living in the world. If we are to follow Christ it must be in our common way of spending every day.'[11] Our baptismal call is to the usually unglamorous but holy engagement with life as lived in the familiar streets and buildings of our local corner of God's world. Most obviously for those called to Ordained Local Ministry, the local situation is the place where our vocation is nurtured, identified and tested, and where it is to be lived in the future. It can be a challenge to be the local person who is ordained – there is no room for mystique or pulling the wool over people's eyes: they know us too well for that. There is also the challenge of transformation, of growing before people's eyes, and of leading them along the same path so that they too grow in holiness and love of God. This may involve rocking the known status quo which we buy into simply by being a local resident. In contrast, deacons who move into a new area have the seeming advantage of coming without a known history, although this can be a trap for the unwary if it proves to be a temptation to avoid the demands of engaging incarnationally and with honesty. Whether on familiar or unfamiliar ground, deacons face the challenge of incarnational living that holds in tension deep engagement in life and the critical distance that enables us to ask hard questions of the familiar and then to bring theological resources to bear on them.

Kathleen Norris, returning (as a lay person) to the small town in Dakota where her grandparents had lived and were in everyone's memory, had to learn to make the place her own too. She describes it as her 'spiritual geography, the place where I've wrestled my story out of the circumstances of landscape and inheritance'.[12] In my own case, moving to a former steel town in the rust belt of the United States from southern England opened me to the relentless demands of wrestling my story out of this new environment which never quite felt like home, however hard I tried to make it so. It was encapsulated for me (with a town planning background) in the drab townscape; other people will have their own focus for the wrestling. Slowly as I struggled with the dereliction, the drugs and the crime, and with my sense of alienation, it began to be familiar and thus part of me, to acquire its own unique sense of place in my life as I got to know some of its people's stories and to make my story part of the town's story. It became the context for my discipleship and encounter with God, and occasionally it surprised me. At that time I did not know the poetry of the Irish priest Padraig Daly. He puts into words the experience I was feeling my way towards, in his case as he saw the presence of God in grey-rendered council houses that could be anywhere yet are vividly specific in our imaginations:

If God is anywhere,
He is rapturously here, early at morning,
In the grey of an English Council Estate:

The skies hold back the rain,
Bins stand in squat order,
Buses move gravely from stop to stop.

Cats forage on a green
Littered with bottles and empty cans,
Crows quarrel for the remains of battered fish;

Doors open,
Faces emerge
To the icy touch of day.[13]

Once I was ordained, I had to make a new American small town a part of me and I am not sure how far I succeeded, although gradually I got a grasp of some local history and began to untangle the network of relationships in a town where everyone seemed to be someone else's cousin, and the grapevine was ferocious in its efficiency. Again, Kathleen Norris helps to put this into perspective:

Allowing yourself to be a subject of gossip is one of the sacrifices you make, living in a small town. And the pain caused by the loose talk of ignorant people is undeniable. . . . Like the desert tales that monks have used for centuries as a basis for theology and way of life, the tales of small-town gossip are often morally instructive, illustrating the ways ordinary people survive the worst that can happen to them; or, conversely, the ways in which self-pity, anger, and despair can overwhelm and destroy them. Gossip is theology translated into experience. . . . When we gossip, we are also praying, not only for them but for ourselves. At its deepest level small town gossip is about how we face matters of life and death.[14]

Stories and gossip are building-blocks in ministry. We will be the subject of gossip as others observe us, just as gossip can inform our ministry – deacons have their ears to the ground but should also be known as trustworthy people who can keep confidentiality. For many people, whether in a small town, an inner city, or deeply rural areas, the only things they will learn about God are from what they see in our lives. And if we ignore the places where they live, what will they learn? Ben Quash makes some interesting observations about this, emphasizing the importance of the local church's engagement with the local scene:

If you arrived in England from another planet and wanted a description of the truth of the nation's life, and you read the national papers to find such a description, little would indicate to you that the Church played an important role in the nation. If, on the other hand, you arrived from another planet and decided to begin by reading the *local* papers, you would get a totally different impression, 'Vicar tackles council on care for the elderly'. . . . In the local press, the Church's role in community life – providing care, taking responsibility, focusing local activities, and all the rest of it – is described and acknowledged. In this context there is nothing *odd* about the place of the church. . . . In a curious sense, the local priest and the local paper have quite a lot in common. They are both identifiably proficient describers of their locality, and are both people who do their describing on *behalf* of the community. Almost the only time that the national media recognise this local proficiency is when there is some local disaster – a bomb or a rail crash – and then, suddenly, the local priest is interviewed to express the feelings of the locality.[15]

We saw this played out in the tragedy at Soham when the routine, incarnational, day-to-day ministry of the church suddenly came to the nation's attention as the parish priest, whom the media used as spokesman for all the local churches, revealed the depth of the church's engagement in a community caught up in the horrors of kidnapping and murder. What is perhaps overlooked is that fact that they could deal with the appalling because they daily dealt with the routine, unintentionally laying the foundation for the trust in the ministry of the church that was needed in this emergency. Daily diaconal ministry, unheralded and unsensational, bore fruit that continues long after the media left.

In a not widely available poem, 'Look',[16] R. S. Thomas articulated the challenge of finding and keeping faith in the midst of life that is harsh in an environment we cannot control. In a bleak farming environment he wrote vividly of dipping belief in seas of manure, and of people squelching through this. This is dramatic language. What does belief dipped in manure look like? Diaconal ministry will involve dipping not just our toes but our belief in our particular local manure, whatever that is. And it may not be pretty. Until that has happened we may not be able to understand local people. It is the fruit of incarnation, and it is our responsibility to know and to name the seas of manure before God and the church, which may want to close its eyes at this point, and then to be prepared to act on behalf of those who squelch in them. Unlike most other dedicated professionals, clergy do not go home elsewhere at night so are well placed to articulate the local story, to use words the community can own, as here in R. S. Thomas's poem 'The Word':

A pen appeared, and the god said:
'Write what it is to be

man.' And my bare hand hovered
long over the bare page

until there, like footprints
of the lost traveller, letters
took shape on the page's
blankness, and I spelled out

the word 'lonely'. And my hand moved
to erase it; but the voices
of all those waiting at life's
window cried out loud: 'It is true.'[17]

It is the particular ministry of the deacon to be the eyes and ears of the church in the local area, observing, engaging, interpreting, praying. Only so could Thomas have known to write 'lonely' and thus heard the chorus of affirmation from the voices around him. The deacon, charged with bringing the pastoral ministry of the church to those in need, seeking out the lonely, the forgotten, the sick, the marginalized, those in trouble, will become an expert in the geography of need in the local area and thus will know the apposite word to use. We can all draw mental maps of our area, putting down the landmarks that are significant to us, and it should be expected that a deacon's mental map will include the places of despair, but also of hope as he or she sees Christ in the midst of the life of the world, catching and naming the glimpses of God appearing in the cracks of life.

I never acquired an American accent, but soon learned that there were words and phrases I had to use instead of my own if I was not to be misunderstood either comically or with more serious consequences. The same is true of cultures within our own society; we may not be able to identify with them so strongly that we 'acquire the accent' but we must be able to hold an intelligible conversation. Thus there is wisdom, as well as frequent necessity, in the practice of giving the newly ordained deacon the youth club to run. Young people can be relied on to open the eyes of their elders to worlds that most adults might never otherwise inhabit, and they give lessons for free in learning another language and culture, thus laying the groundwork for future ministry. Similarly, I think of one of our

students who, with some trepidation, entered the unfamiliar territory of an asylum centre and was immersed in a world she never
dreamed could exist in this country, and determined to become an
advocate in her church and local area for the asylum seekers. Having displayed the outgoing, risk-taking and world-oriented perspective that diaconal ministry requires, she is discovering what Dietrich
Bonhoeffer wrote about before his death at the hands of the Nazis:

> It is only by living completely in this world that one learns to have
> faith. . . . this is what I call this-worldliness – living unreserv-
> edly in life's duties, problems, successes, failures, experiences and
> perplexities. In doing so we throw ourselves completely into the
> arms of God, taking seriously, not our own sufferings, but those
> of God in the world – watching with Christ in Gethsemane. That,
> I think, is faith, that is *metanoia,* and that is how one becomes
> human and a Christian. How can success make us arrogant, or
> failure lead us astray, when we share in God's sufferings through
> a life in this world?[18]

The beauty of the world

We engage with the world in its suffering and need, but we also
engage with the world in its beauty and ecstasy. That is the essential
other side to diaconal ministry; without it we will burn out and our
ministry to others will always be tinged with sadness. The luxury of
sheer joy in God's world is ours and we can give ourselves and our
congregations permission to wallow in it. This, too, demands attentiveness of us. Gerard Manley Hopkins caught glimpses of God's
presence in creation and records this in his poems and his journals.
'Nothing is so beautiful as spring', he declared, and went on:

> What is all this juice and all this joy?
>   A strain of the earth's sweet being in the beginning
> In Eden's garden.[19]

On 3 May 1866 Hopkins saw 'Sky sleepy blue without liquidity'
and 'cowslips capriciously colouring meadows in creamy drifts',
and on 24 September 1870 he saw the Northern Lights for the first
time and recorded the experience in his journal, concluding:

This busy working of nature wholly independent of the earth and seeming to go on in a strain of time not reckoned by our reckoning of days and years but simpler and as if correcting the preoccupation of the world by being preoccupied with and appealing to and dated to the day of judgement was like a new witness to God and filled me with delightful fear.[20]

Hopkins knew how to look and how to be nourished by what he saw. Similarly, writing of Thomas Traherne's work, Graham Dowell sums up his world-affirming approach, which can be ours in diaconal ministry, that embraces the world in its misery and its majesty, expecting to find God there:

> Whereas advocates of Via Negativa, from Thomas à Kempis to the Puritans, with their anti-rational pietism, sharply divided nature from 'supernature' and encouraged withdrawal from the world with its snares and distractions, Traherne in his search for Felicity made a full affirmation of this world in all its beauty and variety. His is the spirit of St Francis who gave himself wholly to God and so to all his creatures, finding communion with them and, in the special relationship which he seems to have enjoyed with the natural world, a way to deeper communion with God.[21]

When were we last moved by beauty into encounter with God? Are we open to such experiences? How do we hold together the wonder and the worry of our world? Do we engage with the physicality of God's world in daily employment or in our hobbies? Esther de Waal writes of the Benedictine insight that manual work is a constant reminder of the incarnation, but it is manual work that is kept in proportion by prayer and study.[22] We are challenged to hold everything in creative tension, to live with paradox and with conviction as we engage with God's world. Faced as we are with a needy and corrupted world, it is so easy to be overwhelmed into a feeling of insignificance and hopelessness, losing the eschatological perspective that is a concomitant of the incarnation. We must be people who live with the perspective of a long timescale but who know the urgency of the present time. I have pondered frequently the challenge given by Joan Chittister that we should take our smallness lightly but our presence seriously.[23] She spoke from the experience of her

Benedictine community's close involvement with the poor and with peace issues. Deacons, with their ministry in both the world and the church, can help the church to live with a light yet serious touch in God's world. The world needs the ministry of deacons who will lead the church by example in Christ-like engagement with the world.

3

The Deacon at the Margins

God's marginal work

If the incarnation is central to diaconal ministry, one consequence is that deacons will find themselves in most unlikely places, simply because God is there. The margins are God's territory, and one of the persistent themes of the Old Testament is the struggle of the people to understand that God was not confined to their safely circumscribed territory. When the people went into exile, they learned that God was there too – they were not abandoned, not without hope. When they did return home it was with their theology forever upset by the experience of living on the margins of their known world.

This upsetting continued in the life and ministry of Jesus. The Gospel writers do not give us a neat picture: he ate with rich and poor, socialized with the powerful and the outcast, spoke with Jew and Gentile. It would be so much tidier if he'd chosen only one of each pair, at least then we could categorize him, but instead his actions challenge us at every turn. Instead he held together hospitality with those on society's margins and those at its centre, defying any attempts to sideline people on the margins. This is our example for diaconal ministry.

Looking to Jesus and hearing his words from a hermeneutic of marginality implies a two-fold acknowledgement. First it sees Jesus' ministry as focused on the margins and on the radical re-ordering of present reality. Second, it recognises and 'names' the experience of God at the margins. More succinctly: to view the word and the work, the meaning and message of Jesus in this way is to attend to the presence and action of God manifest in the margins as well as in the lives of those who manifest God's Spirit there.

What is the view of Jesus that emerges when one looks and hears from the margins? One might say that it is the *kenosis*, the self-emptying, of Jesus Christ described by Paul.[1]

Because God has taken human flesh, has become a God of the margins, life as we knew it has been turned inside out, upside down. We are given previews of this in the Magnificat and the Benedictus when Mary and Zechariah sang of topsy-turvey situations, of the humble being exalted and the mighty being cast down from their thrones. If this is what God is doing, then we can expect our ministry to follow in its wake.

But society as a whole tends to ignore its margins – in the ordination service they are called the 'forgotten corners of the world'. They are often uncomfortable places and the Church can be as good as any other institution at avoiding them. However, the God we worship is the God who is forever out ahead of us, moving into new places, new marginal territory, opening up new pathways and asking us to follow. Philip Sheldrake argues that there is no such thing as inherently sacred space or place but that all space and place has the potential to be a venue for encounter with the holy:

> In the light of incarnation, spirituality is undoubtedly concerned with how to live within the complex world of events. Our place is specified by God's commitment to the particularities of the world and of human history. The event of Jesus Christ is set in a particular time and place. . . . The world of particular places is therefore the theatre of conversion, transformation and redemption. However, Jesus' place is also marked by an empty tomb. 'He is not here, he has been raised as he said . . . indeed he is going ahead of you to Galilee'. God in Jesus cannot be simply pinned down to any here and there, this and that. The place of Jesus is now perpetually elusive. He is always the one who has gone before. To be in the place of Jesus, therefore, is literally to be disciples, to be those who 'follow after' in the direction of Jesus' perpetual departure.[2]

As those who follow in the direction of Jesus' perpetual departure, the Church will find itself living not just in the world but on the margins. Diaconal ministry has to be familiar with this territory and comfortable in it. Deacons need to be able to occupy space on the boundaries, to be liminal people who are at ease alongside people who are on the edges of church and society. Some deacons are equipped by professional qualifications for secular work on society's margins. In the United Reformed Church, diaconal ministry is expressed in the work of Church Related Community Workers (CRCW), who have professional training which includes long-term community placements. Similarly, in the Lutheran Churches of Norway and Sweden, professional qualifications are obtained prior to training as a deacon and many deacons are integrated into the public welfare system. In the Anglican Church professional qualifications are not essential, since a vocation identified within and by the Church is primary, although some diaconal vocations grow out of lived experience of working in a professional or voluntary capacity with people on the margins. What is important, whether or not the deacon has professional qualifications, is the ability to relate to people for whom the mainstream of society is a long way off. In looking for possible diaconal vocations, the instinctive ability to get alongside people of different ages and social contexts and speak their language is an important marker, along with evidence of a life of service outside the Christian community.[3] The Church could be identifying such people among its baptized and asking if this is a pointer to a diaconal vocation.

It is not enough to able to relate to the margins with comfort; deacons are there as God's people, interpreting in language that others can understand that God is there, setting what they hear and see there in the light of the whole revelation of God's ways with the world. Therefore deacons also inhabit the margin of the church and the world, putting the two in dialogue. Bishop Brooke Foss Westcott, 'The Miner's Bishop', wrote in 1887: 'The Church is the prophet of the eternal in the light of creation. . . . The Church is the interpreter of the world in the light of the Incarnation. . . . The Church is the quickener and sustainer of life in the light of the Redemption.'[4] Deacons make connections for the church and the world, speaking theologically of contemporary society, asking how and where God is in this situation, acting to bring about God's life, seeing Christ in the people on the margins (Matthew 25.31–46).

This is intricately linked to worship and in church deacons should destabilize worship so that it moves from the sanctuary to the margins. Centuries ago, Bishop John Chrysostom spoke of this when, teaching about worship and the world, he spoke of the 'other altar composed of the very members of Christ; this very body of the Lord is made your altar . . . when you see a poor brother, reflect that you behold there an altar'.[5]

The Community of Sant' Egidio is a lay Roman Catholic community founded in 1968 and numbering over 50,000 members in 70 countries, dedicated to evangelism and charity. Writing of the lessons learned from it, Monica Attias reflects that

> [Y]ou cannot love Jesus in the Blessed Sacrament and not find him and love him in the poor whom he came to save. . . . Meeting the weakness of the poor has helped us discover the true meaning of being human and being Christian. The lie of self-sufficiency is revealed in our being wholly dependent upon God and not on our own strength. In the Eucharist we are all beggars together at the same table.[6]

This is one good reason why diaconal ministry, to be Christ-like, must embrace ministry on the margins of the world and the church, facilitatating two-way traffic, so that in leading the worshipping community in prayer the deacon ensures the needs of the world take their rightful place and the Eucharist informs our response to the world.

A stable centre

In order to be safe on the margins, we need to be secure in the centre. Therefore diaconal ministry has to flow from a rooted and grounded spirituality centred on God. In Benedictine terms we need both stability and conversion of life. The danger is that of cutting loose from the centre and finding ourselves adrift on the margins with nothing to offer to those we encounter that is distinctively Christian; it is like building a bridge but abandoning the bridgehead. Attention to our own stability is vital and, though the time this takes may seem to be wasted to some activists, we can then live securely with the world's hard and unanswered questions. Dostoyevsky wrote of a 'hosanna born of a furnace of doubt'. In marginal ministry that may be our experience too; the important thing is that we are stable enough to sing 'hosanna' with integrity. John Holdsworth asserts: 'The church is a place where the fundamental questions raised by the possibilities of God's absence can dialogue with the traditions that assert his presence.'[7] For that to be the case in practice the deacon needs to be able to facilitate that dialogue, secure in the tradition of God's presence but not threatened by God's seeming absence. Theological training and pastoral wisdom are essential, but so are those psalms that were first prayed in marginal territory as the Psalmists tested their faith in words and emotions that cross the centuries. Psalm 109, with all its anger and raging words (many of them, it should be noted, not directed at God but being the words of others reported to God), and Psalm 59, with its descriptions of enemies as howling dogs and trap-layers, may not sound like words that automatically belong in church. But what if we use them in our prayers for an old lady trapped in a tower block by broken lifts and drug addicts in the stairwells, or asylum seekers who are hounded by racists? Then they not only give us words to pray for those on the margins, but can also help to stabilize us in God as we deal in prayer with both the presenting need and our own reactions.

Belden Lane's fascinating book, *The Solace of Fierce Landscapes*, explores life on the boundaries both physically – he loves mountains and wild places – and emotionally as he accompanied his mother through her long last illness in a nursing home. He draws widely on the Christian tradition as well as his own observation as he searches for ways to dwell on the margins. In so doing he has insights for diaconal ministry where both engagement and distance are needed. He writes of the holy men and women who inhabited the deserts of the Middle East, who lived and prayed on the physical and emotional margins, and who were sought out for their wisdom. For them the margins were places to pursue God as well as places from which to gain perspective as they ministered to others. Their example raises questions for us as we minister at the margins.

> The holy man in late antiquity functioned on the edges of society, serving as mediators of conflict. . . . People [looked] to the desert monk for the kind of even-handed guidance only possible from someone wholly disengaged from the world. . . . The desert provided the necessary platform from which the holy man or

woman could objectively assess and mediate tensions emerging
in the world from which they had withdrawn. . . . Refuge in the
desert, therefore, was mandatory. Yet just as important was an
angle from which the world now abandoned could also be viewed
in broad perspective. Prospect, too, was required.[8]

This was not solitary escapism, there was also a common life
among the desert monastics, and in the desert they learned what
Rowan Williams describes thus: 'Not some individual technique for
communing with the divine, but the business of becoming a means
of reconciliation and healing for the neighbour. You "flee" to the
desert not to escape neighbours but to grasp more fully what the
neighbour is – the way to life for you, to the degree that you put
yourselves at their disposal in connecting them with God.'[9] Thus
John the Dwarf said, 'you don't build a house by starting with the
roof and working down. You start with the foundation . . . the
foundation is our neighbour whom we must win. The neighbour is
where we start. Every commandment of Christ depends on this.'[10]
Diaconal ministry is meaningless without the neighbour.

Deacons do not move literally to the desert (although a regular
retreat helps), but metaphorically we may be driven or led there.
We may be baffled or disorientated, since that may come with the
marginal territory. But, like the holy people of old, we should be
mature enough to acquire prospect and perspective from this vantage
point. Formation for diaconal ministry may involve coming to terms
with bewilderment and knowing how to grow through it. Some of
my deepest learning and formation has been in situations which felt
like uncharted territory, where there were no easy answers and life
had to be lived with an element of provisionality. It was through
them that I discovered new aspects of my stability in God, as well
as what I believed about the situation concerned. The early desert
father Abbot Poemen told his disciples that it is not what happens to
us that causes stagnation in the Christian life, but not understanding
what has happened that holds us back from moving forward.[11] This
need to find and hold our centre in the midst of marginal ministry
requires the support and counsel of a wise spiritual director; we
cannot go it alone.

There is no inherent merit in living on the margins, and deacons
cannot go in for heroics to bolster their image. Instead, what matters

is how we live there. Real marginal territory can be unnerving, forcing us both inward onto our own resources and outward towards mutual dependence on others who are with us. Marginal territory is not romantic, even when it happens to be beautiful; it may appear harsh, even ruthless. The margins are often indifferent to their inhabitants and survival there requires inner stability, another reason why diaconal formation is so important and why worship is at the heart of diaconal life. Although the margins may make us uncomfortable, if we can be fully present, fully alive, there then they can become fruitful places, life can blossom there and others will find, like Jacob, that 'surely the Lord is in this place and I did not realize it' (Genesis 28.16).

Ministry on the margins

Having spoken about a stable centre, paradoxically deacons cannot minister on the margins if they are unwilling to be de-centred for themselves and to move away from the security of the church. In saying this, we must recognize that any experience we – who *choose* to move in that direction – have on the margins cannot be the same as that of those people who *have* to be on the margins. It is not the same thing to choose poverty and to have poverty forced upon you. When I lived in the US in a religious community we chose to live below the poverty line, and although there were similarities in experience with our neighbours we had choices and shared resources that could never be open to those for whom this poverty was their world for life. That experience of shared ministry still challenges me about the potential for the Church to think more boldly: rather than having one deacon working on the margins, establishing teams with deacons as catalyst and theological resource people for the ministry of the whole Church. Some churches already have teams working on the margins, for example, the ecumenical Alabaré project in Salisbury – led by a Roman Catholic deacon – reaches out to a variety of vulnerable people.

Ministry at the margins will demand that we develop the tenacity to keep on speaking for those who cannot speak for themselves, or who do not know how to make themselves heard. This is the beginning of prophetic ministry, the 'telling how it is' that characterized

Amos and some of his peers and which must not be daunted by the fact that the powerful may not see things this way and may deny the truth of what needs to be said. Such speaking requires courage and requires that we first listen with courage, perhaps to what we do not want to hear. Listening is paramount for a deacon. Being aware of being heard may be so unfamiliar an experience for some people that simply listening to them is profound ministry. Developing the skills to listen well to what is said and what is not said, to the subtext, ought to be a part of all diaconal training. Only then can we learn how to speak what may, at first, seem unfamiliar to us, since 'empowerment requires listening to the language of grief and lamentation so that we can learn to speak it to others. From the perspective of the margins, the old order is passing away; those at the centre must grieve its loss.'[12]

The language of grief and lamentation cannot be divorced from the prophetic word that tells the truth about life. The biblical record is that those prophets who protested most were also the prophets who lamented most. Today most people have lost the art of lamentation; instead we expect to be able to fix things and to apportion blame – if there is any doubt about this, a morning's listening to *Today* will settle the matter as the search for culpability is conducted relentlessly on our airwaves and the possibility of lamenting in the face of the mystery of tragedy seems to be discounted. Deacons are grievers and lamenters, because they move among people who grieve and lament. However, they do not grieve and lament without hope, and the fact of their presence there as deacons of the Church is a tangible sign of a hope that is not simplistic but has its roots in the fertile soil of the Paschal mystery, that out of death God brings life. To do this requires that we are not identical with the marginalized, but are identified with them. In Dan Hardy's words, the Church is charged with mediation that requires

> placing the intensity of the gospel in the closest affinity to those lives and societies to which it is addressed. This may well require critical distance from them and prophetic engagement with them but that distance from those to whom the gospel is addressed must not arise from limited sensitivity to others and their needs. Those who mediate must be close to those to whom they address themselves, thinking their thoughts in order to find the intensity

of the gospel in their forms of life, and expressing the gospel in a manner that touches the deepest aspects of their lives. The same issues appear where the forms of Christian life and worship need to match the deepest needs of the world.[13]

That last sentence contains a particular challenge for deacons in their responsibility for worship as they weave life and liturgy together. Outside the context of worship, the church will find that it has many partners on the margins. Given the description of diaconal ministry being advocated here, it is interesting to read an article from a town planning journal about community development workers in a neighbourhood. There are many similarities:

> [Community development workers] are expected to support and stimulate effort. They are concerned with a spectrum of social and economic – and often environmental – [issues] working through problem solving and inter-agency collaboration. L. P. Hartley's novel, *The Go-Between*, offers another description: fulfilling an intermediary function, acting as a junction box to bridge the concerns of people and the capacity of external agencies to respond to them.
>
> A community development worker is the stylus or needle where a local community is the record and the outside agencies are the record player. In the terminology of community action, this is the point at which top down direction can productively meet grass roots action. . . . Continuity is crucial. Regeneration stands a better chance of continuation if the community is left in charge after the end of the formal initiative. . . . 'It is a myth that people aren't interested in getting involved, but they need support and encouragement to do so,' says Trisha Bennett of Bracknell Forest Borough Council. 'That's where development workers come in. We won't do it for you, but we can help you to do it yourself.'[14]

This could work well as a description of part of diaconal ministry but with the additional church-ward dimension of diaconal ministry, the dimension that means the deacon will not let the church off the hook, either by doing all the work for the church or keeping the church in ignorance both of the need and the gospel imperative to respond. We are to speak out about what we find, and thus come back to the charge given by the Bishop to deacons: 'They are to serve the community in which they are set, bringing to the Church the needs and hopes of all the people. They are to work with their fellow members in searching out the poor and weak, the sick and lonely, and those who are oppressed and powerless, reaching into the forgotten corners of the world that the love of God may be made visible.' An earlier version of this charge included the words: 'You are to search out the careless and indifferent . . .' Here was a recognition that there can be an element of carelessness and indifference that has led people to the margins – not just of those in need but perhaps the carelessness and indifference or complacency of those for whom life is so good there is no apparent need for God, or the carelessness and indifference of society as a whole. Diaconal ministry is needed too among the rich and powerful, both to challenge them with the needs of the poor and also among those for whom the glamour papers over the loneliness and need.

Whether surrounded by wealth or poverty, when we are in marginal lands we cannot lose sight of the fact that this is home for some people. It is not a transitory passing place, but the place where they live either precariously or with tenacity. It is therefore a home for the ministry of the church.

The margin of church and world: crossing the threshold

> Do you want to know his name?
> It is forgotten. Would you learn
> what he was like? He was like
> anyone else, a man with ears
> and eyes. Be it sufficient
> that in a church porch on an evening
> in winter, the moon rising, the frost
> sharp, he was driven
> to his knees and for no reason
> he knew. The cold came at him;
> his breath was carved angularly
> at the tombstones; an owl screeched.

PART 2

THE SHAPE OF DIACONAL MINISTRY

4

The Deacon and the Liturgy

Liturgy and life

Worship is central to the identity of the church. We need to worship, to stand in awe, lost in wonder, love and praise, aware of the holiness of God, and thus of our identity as God's people. Worship is the context and catalyst for transformation as the church comes before God. Archbishop Michael Ramsey quoted William Temple's comment that it is sometimes supposed that conduct is primary and worship tests it, whereas the truth is that worship is primary and conduct tests it.[1] He also observed that the deepest initiation in Eastern Orthodoxy comes not from the texts of the fathers but from sharing the liturgy, and the deacon is the guide into the liturgy.[2] Before anything else deacons are worshippers. Only thus can the deacon be a guide into the liturgy. Worship led by a non-worshipper will be a performance.

We do, indeed, assemble in buildings to worship, but the deacon is the constant irritant to anyone who thereby supposes that daily life is left at the door when we enter, or that worship ends with the dismissal; it merely changes location and expression. Liturgy is radically related to how we live our lives, how we fulfil our baptismal vocation, how we offer God our souls and bodies to be a reasonable sacrifice; it means the 'work of the people' and the people should work, aided by the deacon. Liturgy offers us the words, 'Send us out by the power of your Spirit to live and work to your praise and glory', and, 'Go in peace to love and serve the Lord', both of which seem tame compared to the specificity of dismissals which spell out how we should do this, but are nevertheless an inescapable commission. Deacons challenge us to live those words on Monday morning.

Therefore, as part of both the liturgical and catechetical ministry, the deacon should be trained to help people understand that,

> When we are unaware of the social implications of the liturgy, or ignore those implications, we fail to that extent to offer ourselves to God as a 'reasonable, holy, and living sacrifice.' For each time we receive the Body and Blood of our Lord, we are by that act sent to be witnesses to Him before the world. This does not mean that we are to lead pious lives, but that we are to be in the thick of the struggle for justice and freedom and peace.[3]

> Once we comprehend the full import of th[e] doctrine of 'incorporation in Christ', some tremendous implications for our lives will open out to us. What will it do, for example, to our missionary responsibilities when we realise that we not only proclaim Christ's redemptive work in the liturgy, but we offer our own souls and bodies with His in the very same work? And what sort of a social order shall we be content with after we experience a community in which the elements of food and drink are provided and blessed at Christ's table?[4]

The deacon keeps the mission of the church alive in worship. There is a challenging question to be asked of liturgy, 'Where are the verbs?'[5] Alan Webster makes the critique that '[m]ost English liturgies, ancient or modern, lack the language which can inspire our concern for street children, the impoverished or victims of sex tourism'.[6] This is a more specific version of Kenneth Leech's lament that 'liturgy and social justice have been driven apart. So our official formularies do not at all express what needs to be said and done in this area.'[7] Deacons are there to ensure that worship is both heavenly and earthly, to hold liturgy and social justice together and to open people's eyes to the endless possibilities for worship to affect the way we live, and thus to be expressed in the hundreds of different places in which the congregation end up during the week before being summed up again in the liturgy when the church next gathers in one place.

The deacon and public prayer

With the pace and pattern of life today it is unrealistic to expect people to spend long hours in church. Benedict, in fact, wants prayer in community to be brief.[8] The deacon therefore can help to ensure that when people do assemble together for worship, the time is well and life-changingly used, that the liturgy nourishes the common prayer of the church and of individuals who worship. That affects both the way the deacon participates in worship (always on duty, so constantly attentive to what is going on) and the lead he or she gives to others, aware that many come with burdens and needs that the liturgy, if conducted well, can address. Indeed, liturgy can be the most pastoral gift the church offers people as they are carried by and with the congregation into the presence of God.

To lead public prayer is both privilege and responsibility. The ministry of a deacon can be vital in the worship of the congregation, not necessarily doing it all but ensuring, through training and careful behind-the-scenes work as well as visible leadership, that it happens well. We can all recall some less than glorious moments in worship, but they should not be regular features of any church's life, particularly where the problem is avoidable. Benedict insists: 'Monastics will read and sing, not according to rank, but according to their ability to benefit their hearers.'[9] In congregations 'rank' might be replaced by 'enthusiasm' or 'the fact that they have always done it'. Those who lack the gifts or the ability to prepare properly can distract by their ineptitude, thus drawing embarrassing attention to themselves, but those with great gifts may show off or perform – I remember an elderly pianist who commandeered the piano at a conference and played so elaborately that no-one could tell where to begin singing or how to keep the tune. A concert performance is not appropriate in worship. Our worship leadership is not to satisfy our own need to be involved or to showcase our talents, it is to use and hone our gifts so that the church may worship in the beauty of holiness. Deacons need to work at worship leadership gifts for themselves and help others to develop them. What is at stake is the formation of the people of God.

In some churches today worship is planned and led by a team of people, both ordained and lay. The results can be a wonderful expression of the shared ministry of the whole body of Christ or

an opportunity for difficulty, particularly where the people concerned have not been trained to do the task being asked of them.
Deacons have a role here particularly, given their responsibility to
bring the needs of the world to the church, in helping people to pray.
Leading the intercessions is not simple – it is not the same as saying
one's personal prayers in public, although at times it can sound like
it when the congregation is left in the position of eavesdropping
on someone else's prayers that they cannot make their own as a
corporate prayer. Worse are prayers that give rise to the observation that 'most intercessions have more in common with personal
therapy than with baptismal formation'.[10] Contrast that with well-
planned prayers that give voice to the desires of the whole body, that
flow from an understanding of this particular congregation, at this
particular time, in this particular place, and yet also express the fact
that this gathering is part of the universal Church. Good liturgy enables people from diverse backgrounds to identify with the prayers
offered by the whole Church. Teaching others to pray in public is
true diaconal ministry.

Indeed, 'doing the intercessions' is not a mere task, but an out-
flowing of life before God. Richard Hooker, the sixteenth-century
Anglican divine, had much to say about prayer, including the impact
of the priest's personal life on the common prayer of the congregation, since he (and it was he) 'standeth and speaketh in the presence
of God for them. The authority of his place, the fervour of his zeal,
the piety and gravity of his whole behaviour must need exceedingly
both grace and set forward the service he doth.'[11] Do our lives grace
and set forward our service when we lead others in prayer? The
depth of our own prayer life is shown up in the way we lead public
prayer, in the way we approach and address God, in the blending of
praise and intercession, awe and anticipation, grief and gratitude.
We need to work with ourselves, our voices, our natural gifts and
to pursue the best that we can be, seeking help if necessary. Writing
to his clergy in Ely in 1692, Bishop Simon Patrick exhorted them to
give attention to

possessing our minds with a deep sense and feeling of the majesty
of God to whom we speak, and of our great need of the things
which we pray him to bestow upon us. This will naturally compose
our countenances, and regulate the tone of our voice, and make us

pronounce the prayer as gracefully as we would a petition to the greatest majesty on earth. The organs of speech indeed in several men are of a very different frame and figure, so that all cannot speak no more than sing alike; but some more harshly, some more sweetly. Yet an awful sense of God upon our minds, and an hearty love to him, would form every man's voice to as good an accent as his natural capacity will permit.[12]

This was written at a time when the person leading the prayers read them from the Book of Common Prayer. Today we make greater demands since there is scope to write the prayers, and thus it is not just our tone of voice and our countenance that makes or mars the leadership of public prayer. The person charged with this responsibility needs to be fully engaged in the church and fully engaged in the world, so that the way the prayers of the people are crafted, the subject matter chosen and poetic phrasing and expression given to them, the punctuation inserted and the resulting rise or fall of the voice all reflect the sensitivity to God and the world that are integral to diaconal ministry. As David Stancliffe summarizes it: 'It is this interaction between Christ and his people and all that they bring with them that should shape the Prayers of the People, a skilful task of sifting, discernment and concise expression traditionally entrusted to that liturgical go-between, the Deacon.'[13] Michael Ramsey noted the challenge particularly to those who pray and lead prayers in beautiful buildings where the temptation is to forget the world outside: 'The prayer with beautiful buildings and lovely music must be a prayer which speaks from the places where men and women work, or lack work, and are sad and hungry, suffer and die. To be near to the love of God is to be near, as Jesus showed, to the darkness of the world. That is the "place of prayer".'[14]

George Herbert, the seventeenth-century priest and poet, whose brief ministry in Bemerton near Salisbury has borne great fruit through his writings, set high standards for himself and his people, not least in prayer. Here Izaak Walton, who wrote some of the first biographies in English, describes Herbert's approach to public and private prayer. It shows his practical concern for the congregation to be able to participate fully in the prayers that were spoken on their behalf, and makes a damning observation about the tendency to rush the prayers with the familiarity born not of reverence but of contempt. It also lets us in on the balance in Herbert's life as a minister between public and private prayer.

> And to this I must add that if he were at any time too zealous in his sermons, it was in reproving the indecencies of the people's behaviour in the time of divine services; and of those ministers that huddled up the Church prayers without a visible reverence and affection; namely such as seemed to say the Lord's Prayer or a collect in a breath; but for himself his custom was to stop betwixt every collect and give the people time to consider what they had prayed for and to force their desires affectionately to God, before he engaged them into new petitions.
>
> . . . Mr Herbert's own practice . . . was to appear constantly with . . . his whole family, twice every day at the Church prayers in the chapel which does almost join to his parsonage house. . . . [A]nd his constant public prayers did never make him to neglect his own private devotions, nor those prayers that he thought himself bound to perform with his family, which were always a set form and not long; and he did always conclude them with that collect which the Church hath appointed for the day or week.[15]

There is a balance to be found, particularly for deacons who are in secular employment, between prayer with the family and prayer in the church. There can also be difficulties with the timing of the Daily Offices for those going out to work. What is important is not that we slavishly follow George Herbert, who lived opposite his church and was not rushing to catch a train, but that we establish the disciplined pattern of private and public prayer that will uphold us in our ministry and be a scaffolding for our transformation.

> No sooner had I become a little familiar with the liturgy, priding myself on doing it so well, that it began to seem, after all, a very dull and ordinary thing. I couldn't imagine doing this day in and day out for the rest of my life. The genius of the liturgy, though I hadn't learned it at the time, is its ability to anchor the ordinary in the Psalms' repetitive process of continually reconstituting the world, and us within it.[16]

In that last sentence we see the link between liturgy and life which the deacon's ministry embodies.

The ministry of the deacon in the Eucharist

In the Eucharist the local world intersects with the reign of God and we stand on that threshold, worshipping with all the company of heaven and with the person sitting next to us.

> The Eucharist is not simply a ritual act which has meaning within its own contours. It is a microcosm of a redeemed society. . . . The parish needs to take very seriously the consequences of being a eucharistic community, of living out the eucharistic principles in an anti-eucharistic, anti-communal world. But if worship and prayer shape us fundamentally, at a gut level, then there is no more important act that we can perform than one in which we commit ourselves profoundly and in the depths of our being to equality and community.[17]

In these words, Kenneth Leech sets a theological framework and sets the scene for the deacon's ministry to proclaim by example the consequences of being a eucharistic community that is called to serve. The deacon's role in public worship is as representative person, making visible in the liturgy the diaconal nature of the church. The traditional diaconal vestment, the dalmatic (shaped to fit and not to flap!), the maniple or towel worn over the arm and thus always to hand for use, and the positioning of the deacon's stole over one shoulder and tied out of the way under the other arm, signal the deacon's readiness to serve. The fact that a vested minister is dressed to serve is a visible reminder to the church of its own diaconal ministry, following in the footsteps of Christ. The ministry of the deacon in the eucharistic liturgy is essentially a practical ministry of care, compassion and proclamation and should therefore be all of a piece with the deacon's ministry during the rest of the week. The deacon, with a blend of responsibilities in the world and the church, is a constant reminder that eucharistic worship embraces both heaven and earth, a challenge never to let worship or spirituality become totally other-worldly.

Traditionally, certain roles in the Eucharist have been assigned to the deacon, the origin of which goes back to the early years of the Church. *Common Worship* summarizes these as follows:

> In some traditions, the ministry of the deacon at Holy Communion has included some of the following elements: the bringing in of

the book of the Gospels, the invitation to confession, the reading of the Gospel, the preaching of the sermon, when licensed to do so, a part in the prayers of intercession, the preparation of the table and the gifts, a part in the distribution, the ablutions and the dismissal.[18]

Some of these have very practical origins. For example, in the early Church care of the Gospel scrolls and books was a responsibility not lightly entrusted in the face of persecution so the deacon – who needed to be able to read and had been proven to be trustworthy – stored the Gospels at home during the week, brought them on Sunday to the assembly and read from them. In doing this the deacon acted for and on behalf of the whole baptized community, and we know that some deacons paid for this with their liberty or their lives. Today, the deacon is still entrusted with the proclamation of the Gospel. This includes proclamation in church by reading it, but is not limited to that. In a culture where most people can read and there are Bibles in churches we should not forget that whoever reads the Scripture proclaims the Gospel on behalf of all the baptized community who themselves share that responsibility in daily life.

Several of the deacon's roles fit together to make visible the servant ministry of the church in the world. The deacon who calls us to confession is the deacon who last week sent us out into the world to proclaim the gospel and who knows that we have inevitably slipped up in the course of doing that, and so now invites us to confess together – for we are assembled as one body. In leading the intercessions the deacon brings the needs of the world before the church for prayer, and then leads the church in prayer which scoops up all aspects of life before God. In churches where the deacon has oversight of the pastoral work of licensed lay assistants this is an opportunity to bring to the gathered assembly the varied elements of the church's ministry during the week in which they have been involved, thus giving an ecclesial focus to the work that has gone on in the church's name. Mother Mary Clare describes intercession as not reminding God of his duties but as the church taking a step towards the heart of the world. She adds that we must expect to experience the pain of the world's lack of love for God and of our cruelty to our fellow humans because we cannot escape the responsibility of a world torn by war, discrimination and poverty in the midst of plenty.[19] It is with good reason that one of the things the Church of England looks for in those who are being trained for ordained ministry is quality of understanding and engagement with the world's issues. These are people who can potentially lead us in prayer.

When the president introduces the sharing of the peace by recalling our peace and unity in Christ, it is the deacon who bids the people share a sign of peace, thus linking liturgy and life, giving expression to the truth that has been proclaimed and making preparation to gather around the table as one body. Then, having received the offertory gifts from the congregation – reduced in the West to receiving a plate of monetary offerings but a task that in some countries still includes the very practical business of finding the bread and wine for the Eucharist among the food items offered, and later seeing to the sale or distribution to the needy of anything from bread to live animals – the deacon makes practical preparation of the altar for communion.

After communion the deacon clears up: a very practical and necessary task after a meal. Whilst the soap and hot water part of washing-up after communion takes place later, the fact that ablutions are done straight after the distribution is a very public reminder that the meal is complete, all is consumed and it is time to move on in mission. It is also a sign of stewardship and the practical care we are asked to give to all things that are entrusted to us, since the care we take with the chalice after communion is indicative of the care we take with all the possessions that God gives us. It is a visible reminder that the routine tasks of life belong in worship. And, as Bishop John Taylor reminds us, it reflects God's work: 'Our Creator has been cleaning up the mess, in ceaseless serving love, from the beginning of time, for there is no one else who can do it. . . . God is he who gives himself in love. God is he who pours himself out in service to his world. God is he who is wounded for our healing, broken for our forgiving.'[20]

And finally, the deacon sends us out to love and serve the Lord, gets us over the church threshold and out into the world. The deacon is one of the first over that boundary, greeting people at the door as they leave and effectively leading them out by example. In the early Church deacons had particular duties that exemplified this: they were charged to take communion to the sick and relief to the poor from the offerings of the assembly that had gathered. Today those tasks may be shared with others but they are symbolic of the deacon's role in leading the church in caring ministry in the world. There is a sense in which the deacon embodies John Chrysostom's words that come to us across the centuries: 'Adorn the altar with fine linen if you will, but do not forget your brother who is outside and without a coat. For he is a temple of far greater value.'[21] Speaking to students training for ordination, Myra Blyth referred to the 'act of transition from saying the words to living the sacrament. If we have the rights and privileges to worship in the heavenlies we have the responsibility to come back to earth.'[22]

The deacon in the liturgy is not a free agent, but works with others and thus models the interdependence that is inherent in being together the body of Christ. Normally the deacon does not serve liturgically except with priest or bishop and does not have the focused responsibility of a Reader for preaching, teaching and liturgical leadership. Readers are trained specifically in these areas and most find themselves leading services on their own at times; this will rarely be true of a deacon in public worship on a Sunday. It is a misuse of a diaconal vocation if the deacon finds himself or herself duplicating the ministry of a Reader rather than taking the particular role in liturgy alongside the priest, keeping before the church its own servant ministry flowing from that of Jesus Christ. Aidan Kavanagh points us to the truth, made explicit in the early Church, that it is the deacon rather than the bishop or priest who represents Christ,

> . . . the server of servers, cantor of cantors, reader of readers. He is the butler in God's house, *major domo* of its banquet, master of its ceremonies. Given the service emphasis of his office and ministry, the deacon is the most pronouncedly Christic of the three major ministries. This implies that it is not the Bishop or Presbyter who are liturgically 'another Christ' but the deacon.[23]

Pastoral liturgy

Since the deacon's ministry is not only in church but in the world, he or she is likely to be involved with baptism preparation, marriage preparation and with funerals and bereavement ministry. These pastoral ministries have liturgical expression in church and the deacon is at the heart of them as the church's representative person, able to walk in the shoes of the families concerned whilst also walking in the church's shoes, integrating the joy at the birth of a child with the responsibilities of bringing that child to baptism and fulfilling the baptismal vows; integrating the grief at the death of a loved one with the Christian hope of resurrection. If a deacon's own grief is raw, or their experience of marriage and having children (or not) is painful, he or she has a responsibility to ensure that these needs are being tended to in another context, so that they are not dumped inappropriately on the family concerned.

In baptism, the deacon is the liminal person alongside both the priest and the candidates, accompanying the candidates as they cross the threshold on the last stage of their journey to baptism, alongside them as they are presented and confess their faith (about which the deacon may have taught them), and alongside the priest to welcome them and to charge them to shine as lights in the world.[24] Baptism preparation and bereavement work are long-term events and there is scope for great creativity in the follow-up. The deacon should be free, in a way that the priest may not be free, to devote time to people met through pastoral ministry. Alongside this, the quality of the liturgy may be significant for the wider family and friends attending the pastoral service and the deacon's ability to interpret in the given liturgy the specifics of the family situation is a gift to be developed – the days of generic services mindlessly repeated should be gone for ever. One of our students wrote movingly of a funeral he attended whilst shadowing a hospital chaplain. The deceased was a street person found in a shop doorway, and the student and the chaplain were the only two people at the funeral, but for the student it was one of the most moving services he has attended, giving him new insights into the dignity that should be afforded to a street person in death. This exemplifies Rowan Williams's concern, quoted in Chapter 3, that this man's destiny as a son of God should come to light. The ability to be moved and changed by the services we conduct is a vulnerability we should never lose.

Liturgy can be a safe container for grief and anger, as well as jubilation and excitement, as it holds us before God, giving a framework for setting our experiences in the bigger picture of God's love and good purposes for creation. Good pastoral liturgy gives expression to our perhaps inarticulate or inchoate prayers, but also gently moves us on, not allowing us to become stuck in the depths or the heights of our current experience, keeping it in a perspective that we might not be able to grasp for ourselves. Diaconal ministry in such liturgy is crucial as liturgy blends with pastoral care, and deacons need to develop a liturgical sensitivity to the way it contains and expresses profound personal and corporate experiences before God, as well as God's compassion for us. Not only the shape, words and actions of the liturgy are available to us, but also the liturgical year. My own understanding of death and resurrection hope has been expanded as I have pondered the choice of reading and homily for different people, as I have tried to set this life, this death, in the context of the church's liturgical year: a homily at the funeral of a non-church-going person two days before Christmas sheds a different perspective than one at the funeral of an elderly person of deep faith who died at Easter. The bereaved may only hear 'their' homily, but the minister absorbs them all and should be able to integrate them in his or her life. Sensitivity to the liturgical ebb and flow of the Church year can be an enormous resource that the deacon brings, unobtrusively but with great effect, to liturgical ministry among occasional worshippers who come for a particular service associated with a transition in life. But that sensitivity has to be nourished in the minister's own public and private prayer life. The deacon who has learned to wait in Advent, to rejoice at Christmas and Easter, to repent in Lent, to wonder at Ascension and to be surprised at Pentecost is being equipped to help people bring their daily lives into the story of God's ways with the world.

To go back to where we started in this chapter. Worship is the basic activity and lifeblood of the church; it is primary and our conduct tests it. The deacon is placed at the intersection of the world's life and the church's worship, and is charged with responsibilities to facilitate worship that will enable the church to glorify God and to live as servant in the world. To do this, primarily the deacon must be a worshipper. Added to this is an understanding of the liturgy of the church and of the people who make up the particular worshipping congregation and a commitment to high standards of liturgical leadership. This takes academic knowledge, certainly, but it takes pastoral knowledge that is maturing into wisdom, it takes immersion in the liturgical life of the church undergirded by personal prayer and worship. The deacon as a liturgical person must be a person who understands what is being grasped at here – that liturgy is formative in ways of which the casual worshipper cannot dream, that to be given to liturgical ministry is to set ourselves in the path of constant transformation.

5

The Deacon and Pastoral Ministry

Pastoral ministry in daily life

Eugene Peterson describes a pastor as someone who is 'passionate for God and compassionate with people'.[1] That is a good definition of a deacon and its outworking can be seen in the way a deacon engages in pastoral care, given the charge:

> Deacons are called to work with the bishop and the priests with whom they serve as heralds of Christ's kingdom. They are to proclaim the gospel in word and deed, as agents of God's purposes of love. They are to serve the community in which they are set, bringing to the Church the needs and hopes of all the people. They are to work with their fellow members in searching out the poor and weak, the sick and the lonely, and those who are oppressed and powerless, reaching into the forgotten corners of the world that the love of God may be made visible.[2]

John Henry Newman once said, 'If one does not find God in the vicissitudes of life, where then will one find him?'[3] and the deacon is there to enable this finding and being found to occur. Pastoral care needs to reach into the crevices of life where the world is not as God made it, where people suffer, where creation is abused, where injustice holds sway. So we should expect to find deacons in the thick of the complex issues of our day – asylum centres, street life, drugs clinics, geriatric wards, abortion clinics, pubs and clubs, night shelters and soup kitchens. Deacons need to understand the territory, to be wise in the ways of the world. And they need tenacity if they are to search out and reach into forgotten corners, not just casually look for people in a crowd. The deacon is the eyes and ears of the church in the locality, immersed deeply in life and able to understand what is going on. W. H. Vanstone, whose pastoral ministry and later writings became a source of encouragement and help to many, wrote of his early experience as a curate:

> I arrived in the parish in the autumn: and in the winter evenings which followed I felt the contrast between the monotony and the drabness of the gas-lit streets along which I walked and the rich variety of human activity which was going on so close behind the walls and curtains of scores and hundreds of homes. On the pavements I was never more than three or four feet from someone's living room: and when I visited a house I would step directly from the dismal and usually empty street into the very heart of the life of a person or a family – and there almost anything might be going on, from a family quarrel to the bathing of a new born baby, from an eager game among children to the tending of a dying invalid. I came to think of the long, dismal wall of a row of houses as no more than a façade which was concealing behind it an extraordinary richness and variety of human activity and experience.[4]

This patient engagement in the daily round of life enables the deacon, priest or bishop to make strong connections between the reality of life and the good news of the gospel. Then they can bring the concerns and hopes of the people to the church, whether or not that makes for comfortable listening. Tim Biles, writing out of years of experience of parish ministry, notes that 'Sunday services are not the most important thing in a priest's ministry . . . it is through the ceaseless round of social happenings that pastoral knowledge is built up and pastoral care becomes real to people.'[5] The way a priest learns this is through ministry as a deacon where the emphasis is on incarnational living among people. Sadly there are stories of priests moving to new areas who, in their enthusiasm, turn things upside down immediately with unhappy consequences. David Stancliffe describes deacons in these situations as 'having *the* responsibility to remind the whole Church to engage with reality first, before attempting to transform – or more properly, to let God have the opportunity to transform – our lives'.[6] When ministers engage with patient diaconal work in the ordinary round of life they are equipped in the way Ben Quash describes:

> The parish priest is often in the very privileged position of being able to describe what the truth of everyday life is in a particular

locality. In funerals, he has to describe the truth of a single life. His presence to the locality and to individuals and families authorises this kind of description. The clergy describe well because they are really present to the situations they describe. . . . They have a knowledge which is 'embodied, contextual and personal'. This is a high and precious form of knowledge denied to outside observers, commentators and statisticians.[7]

The deacon has a public, representative ministry and is charged by the church with fulfilling it in the church's name. Michael Ramsey points to this important link between pastoral care and the public ministry of the church when he observes that when a minister visits a sick person it 'is not only the visit of a kind Christian, it is the church visiting'.[8] In some churches where there are lay people trained to share in the ministry of pastoral care offered by the church, the deacon is the person who coordinates their ministry, ensures there is theological reflection on the situations encountered, interprets the needs of the world to the church, and also arranges training for those whom the church discerns could share in this work. However, mindful of the integrative and representational nature of diaconal ministry, Ronnie Aitchison warns of the occasional practice in the Methodist Church of electing a lay deacon to fulfil diaconal ministry for the church: 'What is happening then is that the charitable function as a representation of the love of Christ is disappearing and we drift into welfare work. Herzog finds this an unsupportable situation "separated from *leitourgia*, *diakonia* would become the same as secular welfare work".'[9] Once linked to liturgy and the proclamation of the gospel, pastoral ministry takes on the vision of the reign of God. In doing so it becomes more than reactive care but has the added prophetic dimension born of eschatological hope, and thus challenges the status quo where injustice exists.

Being a compassionate deacon

Michael Ramsey observed that there are people who make God near, and this is the most marvellous thing that one human being can do to another.[10] This is costly ministry and Henri Nouwen writes:

Let us not underestimate how hard it is to be compassionate. Compassion is hard because it requires the inner disposition to go with others to the place where they are weak, vulnerable, lonely, and broken. But this is not our spontaneous response to suffering. What we desire most is to do away with suffering by fleeing from it or finding a quick cure for it.[11]

Most of us know a compassionate person when we see one, and there is more to it than simply doing a task of caring. Compassion makes demands of us, and opens us up in ways we do not anticipate, perhaps revealing depths in us of which we were previously unaware. It involves the inner disposition to go with others to the vulnerable places. But we have to begin with ourselves; unless we take our own hurt and pain seriously we can't take other people's hurt and pain seriously either. Henri Nouwen, who gave up a successful academic career to live and work with people needing continual physical care, described powerfully the way that he found those he cared for physically offered him much more in return, opening up vulnerable places which had remained untouched throughout his earlier career, and offering him joy and community beyond anything he imagined possible.[12] Although we should never engage in pastoral care in order to meet our own needs, especially that invidious need to be needed, and we must be careful never to use other people who have turned to us for our own ends, the truth is that in God's economy we find that God meets with us as we meet with others in God's name. Pastoral ministry can take us into boundary places, not only geographically but also spiritually. In the face of the vulnerability of another person, we too are rendered vulnerable to God. Here one of Mother Teresa's co-workers writes of her experience of the cost of compassion:

> [W]e, as Co-workers, are faced with compassion when we are with the poor and the lonely and the dying. Compassion asks us to go where it hurts, to enter into places of pain, to share our brokenness, fear, confusion and anguish. Compassion challenges us to cry out with those in misery, to mourn with those who are lonely, to weep with those in tears. Compassion requires us to be weak with the weak, vulnerable with the vulnerable, and powerless with the powerless. Compassion means full immersion in the conditions of being human. When we look at compassion this way, it becomes clear that something more is involved than general kindness.[13]

'Compassion means full immersion in the conditions of being human': there is a job description for a deacon. We share the ministry of Jesus Christ who was fully immersed in the conditions of being human, who lived, ate, slept, travelled, laughed and cried with his disciples for three years, who spent thirty years before that with his family in their village (initially Nazareth but perhaps later Capernaum), who endured Roman rule with them, who knew first hand about the suffering of old age, death in childbirth, childhood accidents that crippled for life.

Given this, we are not called to be superman or superwoman, or other people's messiah. The temptation, particularly in the early years of ministry, is always to try to do too much. Timothy Jenkins writes of his experience:

> [A] Christian minister [is] required to pay attention: not to bring God into a situation (as – I am sorry to say – certain of us fresh from theological college had a tendency to believe), but to learn to discern his work and presence in a place. And the other side of that is seeing that you yourself are not necessary to the situation: a clue to discernment is self-effacement. . . . Some young priests tend to flee from their superfluousness, their not being needed, by activism, through being useful. . . . [T]he grace of God is not found fundamentally in uses, or the meeting of needs. Christian worship is – if I may put it so without being misunderstood – thoroughly useless, in the technical sense that it meets no human ends.[14]

A dose of humility, recognition that we are not the only instruments God can use in a situation, can save us from overstepping the mark. Good pastoral care does not force help on another but leaves them in charge and with responsibility; it respects their autonomy and thus their human dignity, and it avoids collusion. Knowing when to stop is as important as knowing when to offer care; being reliable is very different from being omnipresent and perhaps smothering. Eugene Peterson writes: 'Reticence – a healthy respect for limits – is a requisite pastoral skill. An enthusiasm for God's unlimited grace requires as its corollary a developed sensitivity to human limits. We have to know when and where to stop.'[15] This is all simply good practice but it is also theologically a reflection of the way that God works with us, reaching out to us, sharing our life, but leaving us with our autonomy. And so pastoral care may involve us in what feels like rejection or lack of appreciation, and it is our responsibility to handle that appropriately. Michael Ramsey spoke from years of experience when he addressed those who were about to be ordained in Durham:

> Often you will be knowing the joy of seeing men and women and children whose feet have been set, through your ministry, in the ways of God. But also often you will find times of frustration, baffling and mysterious, and in those times when you can see and feel no signs of usefulness or its fruits, you will know in faith, from your nearness to your Lord, that what you are and what you do are being used by him in his love and wisdom. . . . As you strive to be useful you will remember the course of our Lord's mission: thirty years of hidden life, three years of public ministry, and then the waste (as it seemed) of Calvary. Useful priest, there is your exemplar![16]

Padraig Daly's poems are powerful and at times disturbing reflections on his ministry as a priest in Ireland. But, like the Psalmists of old, his questions are directed to God. Here, in a poem called simply 'Ministers', he addresses God with the demands of compassion, perhaps in anger or perhaps in awe:

> It is we who are kicked for your failures;
>
> When pain lasts across the night,
> When people gather helplessly around a bed,
> When grief exhausts the heart,
> It is we who must bear the anger.
>
> When love fails,
> When friends are gone,
> When worlds are rubble,
> When eyes cannot lift to see the sun,
> People ask us to explain; and we are dumb.
>
> When rage against you is a fierce sea
> We are the first rocks on the shore.[17]

We can see similar poetic prayer in some of the prayers of Michel Quoist, the French priest who wrote in the middle of the last century. In *Prayers of Life*,[18] he wrestles with some of the needs he encountered, and the demands they made on him as a man. This was one of the first books on prayer that I read as a teenager and I simply assumed this was the way to pray. With hindsight I am grateful for this early exposure to a model of such honesty in prayer and ministry.

And how can we sustain ourselves in this costly ministry? It is significant that much of the caring ministry of the Church has, over the years, been provided by monastic communities which are grounded in daily prayer. The two are inextricably linked, the common prayer life sustaining the ministry among the needy. But it is not just prayer, it is the encouragement that we offer one another through our common life that matters for our ministry in the world. Here Gerard Manley Hopkins reflects in a sermon on the encouragement Jesus offered to his disciples:

> He loved to praise, he loved to reward. He knew what was in man, he best knew men's faults and yet he was the warmest in their praise. When he worked a miracle he would grace it with / Thy faith has saved thee, that it might almost seem the receiver's work, not his. He said of Nathanael that he was an Israelite without guile; he that searches hearts said this, and yet what praise that was to give! He called the two sons of Zebedee Sons of Thunder, kind and stately and honourable name! ... He said to Peter / Thou art Rock / and rewarded a moment's acknowledgement of him with the lasting headship of his church. He defended Magdalen and took means that the story of her generosity should be told for ever. And though he bids us say we are unprofitable servants, yet he himself will say to each of us / Good and faithful servant, well done.[19]

The reason why this is so significant for Hopkins can be seen in another journal entry: 'Our schools at Roehampton ended with two days of examinations before St Ignatius' feast the 31st. I was very tired and seemed deeply cast down till I had some kind words from the Provincial.'[20] The simple recognition by another person that he was exhausted, and the offering of kind words, was life-giving, and in offering that the Provincial was offering a ministry of encouragement and care, listening for the meaning that lay behind Hopkins's words and body language. Dietrich Bonhoeffer expressed the same thing when he wrote from prison: 'There is hardly anything that can make one happier than to feel that one counts for something with other people. . . . In the long run, human relationships are the most important thing in life.'[21] Another example, which shows why it is so important that episcopal ministry is rooted in diaconal ministry, comes from Archbishop Desmond Tutu's experience of Archbishop Robert Runcie: 'He was friendly, warm and affirming of others and had the happy knack of making the apparently most insignificant and most unprepossessing of us feel important. He made us feel that we really counted, and that whatever our views, for him they were important and were weighed very carefully.'[22]

What is going on here? It takes us back to Evagrius Ponticus, quoted in Chapter 1. There is an attentiveness that sees another's situation, puts it under the microscope to observe the detail, and acts compassionately. There may be particular attention to small things that are observed as being needed – stopping to shake hands, standing in a position for a person to lip read, walking slowly so the other person is not left struggling to keep up, offering praise or encouragement that could go unsaid but is nevertheless articulated. It makes people feel they matter. We have a classic account of this type of diaconal caring ministry in action in Izaak Walton's account of a 'poor old woman' who came to George Herbert. After some explanation of her need,

she was surprised with a fear and that begot a shortness of breath, so that her spirits and breath failed her; which he perceiving, did so compassionate her, and was so humble, that he took her by the hand and said, 'Speak good mother, be not afraid to speak to me; for I am a man that will hear you with patience; and will relieve your necessities too, if I be able; and this I do willingly, and therefore, mother, be not afraid to acquaint me with what you desire.' After which comfortable speech he again took her by the hand, made her sit down by him, and, understanding that she was of his parish, he told her that he would be acquainted with her and take her into his care: and, having with patience heard and understood her wants (and it is some relief for a poor body to be but heard with patience), he like a Christian clergyman comforted her by his meek behaviour and counsel; but because that cost him nothing, he relieved her with money too and so sent her home with a cheerful heart, praising God and praying for him.[23]

Following Jesus' example does not mean that in our enthusiasm to welcome people we ignore what is wrong, perhaps sinful, but we reach beyond the actions to meet the person. Indeed, if there is something wrong then eventual naming and dealing with it as sinful is the unique gift of Christian ministry, since only God in Christ can deal with sin. Here is Sean Connolly, a Roman Catholic priest, on the subject of pastoral ministry:

What, at a day to day level and more than anything else, am I asked to deal with in pastoral ministry? The answer is, I think, sin. . . . What, though, is sin if not a turning away from God at some level or another? And the reality is – for most of us – that we have, at least in part, turned away. Our whole journey consists in being persuaded to turn back around; to face Him and to realise that all we will actually encounter is simply Love itself. It seems to me that most of my priestly, pastoral ministry is ultimately about being privileged to be a part of that ongoing, divine persuasion.[24]

Whilst it is the priest who gives the absolution, it is not without reason that deacons lead people in confession and then in sharing the peace when the reconciled church gathers for the Eucharist.

Underlying all these examples, there is an attitude of heart that deacons can cultivate: the attitude of compassionate hospitality which respects the dignity of every person and provides a still centre where there is space for people to rest. It always comes back to the demanding way of living expressed by St Seraphim, the Russian saint of the nineteenth century: 'Be at peace, then thousands around you will find salvation.' The Rule of the Monastic Community of Jesus in Paris expresses this. Based in the city, the monastics live by a rule which charges them:

Welcome the city. By choosing to live there you welcome its rhythms, laws, problems, tragedies, difficulties and holiness. Bound up like this with its life, your lifestyle and faith should make you credible in its eyes.

The people who surround you, whom you rub shoulders with and receive, who pray with you, are thirsty for living water, tormented with fatigue, anxiety, solitude, anonymity and noise. For their sake, try to create an oasis of prayer and peace.

Silently and gratuitously, welcome the guests that Providence sends to your table. Besides a meal, you offer them a space of calm and peace and your prayer can only be nourished by these contacts.[25]

And lest all this become too serious, a healthy sense of proportion and of the ridiculous, and a lightness of touch with ourselves and others, are indispensable for diaconal sanity as well as for theological balance. Thus Robert Runcie could describe Sister Jane SLG at her funeral in these words:

She did feel that people without a sense of humour lacked a sense of proportion and should never be put in charge of anything – especially a country or a community. While outraged by the injustices of the world, she warned an angry campaigner, 'It is important not to get bogged down in one's impotence to alleviate human misery so that you forget the good things in life that matter so much; lots of people are happy and God is glad for them and with them.'[26]

Vision in pastoral ministry

Because the cross is at the heart of our lives, we will be faced with, rather than protected from, pain and frustration. But at the same time we are people who sing the Magnificat, we are people who hope in God. Diaconal ministry is essentially hopeful. If we do not hope with the assurance that our God comes to save, we might as well not bother. In pastoral ministry we may need to cultivate our ability to hope, since it does not always come naturally. Hope and godly creativity often go hand in hand, because creativity is linked to the ability to envisage a different future and to work towards it beyond the boundaries of the present situation. God is always doing a new thing, always making all things new, and diaconal pastoral ministry takes its vision from that. William Lynch SJ writes that Christianity,

when it is true to itself, proclaims the centrality of wishing and hop-
ing. It is rooted in the Advent ability to wait, patiently but never
resigned, which includes the ability to handle hopelessness. Therefore it will not panic, like a child, at any and every appearance of
the hopeless. [27] Like athletes who hold back until the home straight
while commentators panic and then – knowing their reserves – push
ahead to win, we are to cultivate our reserves of hope, keep pace and
bide our time. We will encounter hopelessness and panic in pastoral
ministry, and at times we will need to take urgent action, but we are
challenged to 'be at peace', praying for ourselves and for the people
we meet for the assurance of the larger place, the spacious place,
that the Psalmist speaks of as God's gift (Psalm 66.12). This hymn
was written for a National Episcopal AIDS Coalition conference on
'Hope and Healing':

> God of hope and God of healing,
> ever turning lives around,
> come restore, come re-inspire us,
> free the hearts that fear has bound.
>
> Hope-filled God, you keep enlarging
> boundaries we try to set;
> raise our sights to new horizons,
> greater dreams than we dream yet.
>
> Healing God, your breath first formed us,
> then, made flesh, our sickness bore,
> here we bring ourselves, our loved ones,
> heal, make whole, breathe life once more.
>
> Author God, you re-write stories,
> turn life's losses into gain,
> hope is known when life seems hopeless,
> health arises from the pain;
>
> so we come with tears and triumphs
> asking you to set us free,
> hope and healing are your nature,
> God of love and mystery.

God of hope and God of healing,
ever turning lives around,
come restore, come re-inspire us,
free the hearts that fear has bound.[28]

Another image of diaconal pastoral ministry is that of the deacon
as midwife, helping to bring new life into the world, understanding
what is going on, knowing the process and thus being able to guide
others through the sometimes fearful times, staying with them, not
doing their work for them but providing the support that is needed
and pointing to the presence of God working in the midst of suffering or grief. I remember vividly a dying woman's poignant words,
'I'm not ready to die, I haven't learned how to live yet', and the
task of accompanying her as she tried to make sense of her past so
that she could face death with peace. My role was to ask the questions that enabled her to tell her story, through tears, and to make
the connections she could not make to the Christian story, using a
picture of the Dominus Flevit chapel in Jerusalem which gave her
the powerful comfort that Jesus, too, wept. Then, miraculously, she
was grasped by the grace to which David Lyall refers:

> In the midst of complexity and ethical ambiguity, the pastoral task
> is not to provide easy answers or to lead people to believe that such
> answers exist (if indeed they ever did). Rather, the pastoral task is
> to 'hold' people in the midst of the complexity and ambiguity and
> to help them catch a vision or to be grasped by a grace which is
> more profound than the easy answer. Effective pastoral ministry
> is a parable of the gospel, pointing beyond itself to the God who
> sustains us and carries us forward in the midst of change.[29]

Deacons, who are sent by the Church to the forgotten corners of
the world, share in an often unglamorous ministry. They know the
truth of Francis de Sales's words, 'Great works do not always lie in
our way, but every moment we may do little ones excellently, that
is, with great love.'[30] To fulfil this ministry, deacons are called to be
faithful in prayer and listening as part of their ministry of pastoral
care and action. Mother Mary Clare describes the challenges:

> Within the silence and the measure of retreat available to all,
> within the discipline of family, community and parish life, given

in all its vigour to God, there must be a listening and attentiveness to God in which the suffering and doubt of humanity are heard more clearly than in the hurly-burly of immediate involvement. In prayer the things of the world are seen in a truer perspective and proportion, because they are seen in the light of God's purpose.[31]

Prayerfulness can protect us from myopia or partial vision, and can lead to vision and thus a prophetic response. The danger is that we are so immersed in situations that we cannot see the wood for the trees, or are numbed to the suffering by over-familiarity. Mother Mary Clare's challenge is to ask whether our prayer life helps us to hear the sufferings of humanity more clearly, and what has happened to our vision of the reign of God. Does the vision of God inform, theologically, our pastoral care? If there is no prophetic element we will always deal with the consequences, not the causes, of suffering. Deacons are to be deeply engaged with the day-to-day pastoral needs they encounter, but alongside this we need a wise engagement with the unjust structures of society, a commitment to environmental issues, and an immersion in local social and political life. The intensity of these engagements will vary, but all deacons need a network of contacts in local life and a wily knowledge of ways round or through the system. To this engagement with the world's manure and mess deacons bring, in the words of the Methodist Church,

> a perceptive, imaginative creative ability to reflect theologically on and in daily life . . . draw[ing] attention to God's presence and activity in the ordinary, surprising and sometimes shocking places and events, often far beyond the identifiable Church. 'Towel and basin' ministries of mess, dirt and menial tasks are revealed as places of encounter with God. Faithfulness to God's calling demands that the Church acts out of its remembrance of Jesus' instruction regarding the washing of feet as well as the breaking of bread. Deacons help focus, represent and enable this calling. Thus the mundane is seen to be the edge of glory.[32]

Because of this and with the help of deacons, the Church can pray and act with hope in words written about the Church's work among people affected by alcohol abuse, remembering that in this – as in all else – the Church, not just the deacon, is the agent of God's healing care.

O God, you see our anguished lives,
the secret pain we bear:
the sudden stab of violence,
the lonely long despair.
We turn for comfort to the things
that bring us further grief,
yet your desire to make us whole
reject in disbelief.

O Jesus Christ, incarnate God,
you suffered in distress,
you know the lonely path we walk,
the pain our tears express.
When silence is a mask we wear,
and, daily, lies unfold,
release sealed lips, let deaf ears hear,
and let the truth be told.

For only truth can set us free,
and love alone can heal,
bring wholeness to our ravaged lives
so hearts long-numbed can feel.
We cry, O God, from terror's depths,
give voice to nameless fears,
abuser, victim, for each one
you wipe away the tears.

Come, soften, strengthen us, O God,
and make your church a place
where sin and sorrow can be named
and fear is touched by grace;
where hope, embodied, brings forth hope,
and courage is revealed,
where lives destroyed, abused and shamed
can be redeemed and healed.[33]

6

The Deacon as Catechist

The scope of catechesis

The Collect for the Ordering of Deacons in the Book of Common Prayer includes the petition, 'Replenish them with the truth of thy doctrine, and adorn them with innocency of life, that, both by word and good example, they may faithfully serve thee in this office', a wise and wonderful request by the Church for its deacons. It holds together in one sentence the fact that the truth of doctrine can replenish us (my thesaurus offers 'stock up', 'top up', 'refill', 'restock' and 'reload' as alternatives, all of which point to the truth of God's doctrine being refreshing and invigorating), that our manner of life can 'adorn' us, and that both our word and our good example are part of our service. Gerald Collins asks, 'What questions about the incarnation can attract the homage of our intellect, and at least indirectly improve our discipleship and inspire our praying?'[1] Have we considered 'the homage of our intellect' as a part of diaconal ministry?

If the role of the deacon in liturgy lies in helping people to worship and to connect world and worship, and the role of the deacon in pastoral care is to be a person of compassion and service, what of the deacon in catechism? Here he or she is called to help people (met in church or in the midst of daily life away from the church) to grow in the knowledge and love of God so that they mature in the faith and live out their baptismal vocation. We are to help people to grow in faith, to be holy, to grow as saints, and in the risky business of living as Christ's disciples. But with that responsibility comes, too, some behind-the-scenes catechism in the deacon's own life:

Deacons are called to work with the bishop and the priests with whom they serve as heralds of Christ's kingdom. They are to proclaim the gospel in word and deed, as agents of God's purposes of love. . . . Deacons are to seek nourishment from the Scriptures; they are to study them with God's people, that the whole church may be equipped to live out the gospel in the world. They are to be faithful in prayer, expectant and watchful for the signs of God's presence, as he reveals his kingdom among us.

. . . You have been ordained deacon in the Church of God: take these Scriptures as a sign of the authority given you today to serve God's people in love and teach them in his name.[2]

The Methodist Church says of its deacons:

[They] never cease to be disciples participating in the worship and mission of the Church along with all other disciples. At the same time their particular vocation leads them in the role of leading, encouraging and equipping others.

The primary purpose in focussing diaconal ministry is to help all Christians discover, develop and express their own servant ministry. Deacons therefore engage in educational and nurturing activities to enable people to see God's activity in daily life and world, and to encourage them in expressing their faith in relevant ways.[3]

A deacon's ministry is not only among Christians; catechesis fits well with the deacon's ministry on the boundary, helping people find their way into church, since much of it is done with those new to the faith and the church. In practical terms it could well include baptism preparation, marriage preparation, inquirers' groups and work with children as they grow in the faith. It is not necessarily preaching, but lays the groundwork upon which preaching can build. Thus, for George Herbert, the role of catechesis is to 'infuse a competent knowledge of salvation in every one of [the parson's] flock' so that preaching can subsequently 'multiply and build up this knowledge . . . [and] inflame this knowledge, to press and drive it to practice, turning it to reformation of life'.[4]

Catechism traditionally includes the element of question and answer. As catechist, the deacon is a person who asks questions in order that others can learn and grow in the Christian faith. Knowing what questions to ask is important. Herbert describes catechism as a process of encouragement and unfolding, using familiar illustrations and rephrasing the question for the person who is struggling so that it contains the answer.[5] Although catechism is essentially oral, the first question any deacon asks should be asked not orally but by the deacon's life as people take note, are stopped in their tracks by what they see. The old saying, 'What you are shouts so loud that I cannot hear what you are saying', is totally applicable to the deacon because other people will not hear our oral questions if they are put off by our lives. It comes back to St Francis's dictum about proclaiming the gospel, using words if we have to.

The seventeenth-century English divines hammered this point home: doctrine and life must match. Jeremy Taylor, writing to the clergy, pointed them to the obligation that came with ordination to live exemplary lives and to the consequences of ignoring this:

> Remember that it is your great duty, and tied on you by many obligations, that you be exemplar in your lives, and be patterns and precedents to your flocks: lest it be said unto you, 'Why takest thou my law into thy mouth, seeing thou hatest to be reformed thereby?' He that lives an idle life, may preach with truth and reason, or as did the Pharisees, but not as Christ, or as one having authority.[6]

Writing a few years later, Henry Dodwell picked up the word 'exemplary' and highlighted two of its characteristics, that it should be excellent and conspicuous. However, arising from this conspicuousness, the public character of the life of the ordained can bring trials of its own which can come as a shock if ordinands and their families have not given thought to this.

> Now because this *Sanctitie of life*, as in you, must also be EXEMPLARY, it will therefore be necessary that it have two qualifications: that it must be EXCELLENT, and that it be CONSPICUOUS.
>
> But on the others side, the convenience of having your Resolutions and several of your Actions known, are: that exposing your self hereby to *publick censure*, you may, *if true*, take them for warnings and admonitions; if false, for trials and exercises of your Patience; that you may therefore terrifie and awe your self into a greater caution, when you remember so many Critical eyes

ready to observe your lapses; that you may avoyd many imperti-
nent temptations which all will be ashamed to motion to a person
unlikely to entertain them.[7]

For Dodwell terror and awe may be the ultimate driving forces
that cause us to be attentive to the way we conduct ourselves; for
Simon Patrick, Bishop of Ely in the 1690s, the motivation was more
gracious and evangelical: care with our lives so that others can be
convinced we believe the excellence of the things we proclaim:

> But above all things we must take the greatest care that our life
> do not contradict our doctrine; for it is not sufficient that our
> conversation in this world be innocent and unblamable, but we
> must endeavour to make it exemplary and useful. It must be so
> ordered as to convince the people that we firmly believe the excel-
> lence of those virtues which we commend to them, and that our
> chief aim and design is to save their souls.[8]

Coupled with this concept that our way of being and living is
integral to the catechetical ministry, there is a distinction between
knowledge and wisdom. The former is useful, but is not a substitute
for wisdom. Knowledge can be gained by education, but wisdom
requires the integration of that knowledge within ourselves. The
French priest Michel Quoist observed: 'Accumulated knowledge does
not make a wise man. Knowledgeable people are found everywhere,
but we are cruelly short of wise people.'[9] Catechism is as much
about formation in wisdom as it is about education. In essence, the
deacon's catechetical ministry is to help people, by living example
as well as words, grow in wisdom and holiness. The root meaning of the word 'education', *educere*, brings with it the meaning of
leading forth or drawing out a person's gifts and potential. This is
in contrast to the concept of education as cramming as many facts
into a person as possible. The emphasis on lifelong learning is now
a part of the culture of the Church through Continuing Ministerial
Education or Development. This is, in fact, not a new issue; here we
have an anonymous author's advice to a newly ordained person in
the early eighteenth century:

> Now the misfortune is, that when we launch out into life, and
> come from the University with the reputation of being well read,
> we are too apt to entertain a mistaken notion, that our studies are

quite finished; whereas, on the contrary, we have yet our greatest exercise to go through, the study of mankind; which speculation cannot ever arrive at, and which is attainable only by mixing with, and mixing among them.[10]

We tend to overlook, as part of our 'study of mankind . . . by mixing with them', the education and training received in 'secular' occupations. One of the gifts that deacons who are Non Stipendiary Ministers (NSM), Ordained Local Ministers (OLM) and Ministers in Secular Employment (MSE) bring to the church is the integration of ordained ministry with life lived in the work place. Wisdom is cultivated in the midst of daily life. Deacons bring to their work, wherever it is undertaken, the wonder that sees and marvels at God's creative work in all the world. Whether it is the mystery of the human body or the precision of a mathematical formula, the educational development of children or the creativity of art, we are daily exposed to, and are learning from, the wonder of God's ways. Given that nearly everyone in church on Sunday will not be there on Monday morning, deacons – whose ministry is in the world as much as it is in church – are to catechize worshippers in godly wisdom wherever they happen to spend Monday morning.

As a specific outworking of this engagement in the life of the world beyond the church door, NSM, OLM and MSE deacons are well equipped to fulfil a particular aspect of the ministry of the deacon which the report on diaconal ministry in the Church of England, *For Such a Time as This*, included within the catechectical ministry of the deacon. This is the task of representing the church's concerns and priorities, on behalf of the bishop, in areas of community action and in relation to major institutions within the diocese (local and regional government, urban regeneration initiatives, the health service, the world of education, the voluntary sector, etc.).[11] Deacons who have particular expertise in these fields are well placed for this ministry, or – using their knowledge of the systems that operate in these areas – to help others to engage in them. Too often the Church, in its past emphasis on stipendiary ministry as normative, has failed to draw on the skills and resources of people who are able to speak to and within the systems of our common civic life. If a deacon works in one of these areas, that may be a sign that his or her particular ministry will embrace this aspect of representing the church's concerns to the authorities as well as taking them to the church for prayer and action.

All this does not preclude intellectual study; indeed, we are commanded to love God with all our minds (Matthew 22.37) and the Psalmist prays that God will test his or her heart and mind (Psalm 26.2, cf. Jeremiah 17.10). As deacons we can expect God to do this, otherwise we cannot be faithful catechists. But in all this, catechism divorced from formation in the love of God is catechism that has lost its bearings. The medieval mystic, Julian of Norwich, said: 'Truth sees God: wisdom gazes on God. And these produce a third, a holy, wondering delight in God, which is love.'[12] Some of the greatest theological writings are essentially prayer and the more we study God's ways, the more awed we should be as their immensity and complexity are revealed to us. The Psalmists are among the biblical writers whose insights into God's world and word led to wonder and adoration (for example, Psalms 8; 106.1–2), and we follow in their footsteps. Evelyn Underhill has a pithy observation about how we are moved in this way, when she writes: 'Wonder and love are caught, not taught; and to catch them we must be in an atmosphere where we are sure to find the germs.'[13] So where is an atmosphere in which we will all be infected? Deacons need to be there.

Being a catechist

According to the charge given by the bishop, catechism involves collaborative ministry with others who are similarly called to be ambassadors for Christ. What is an ambassador? One who is sent by someone else, given authority to speak and act on their behalf, to further that person's interests. There is no such thing as a freelance ambassador, answerable to no-one else. There is no such thing as a freelance deacon. We are in a shared ministry with authority given by God, with fellow workers who are similarly charged with responsibilities to share in the ministry of Christ. The way we relate to one another and share collaboratively in the ministry entrusted to us is part of the question that our lives should ask of the people we are among. The close link between the bishop and the deacon has already been noted. With the emergence of team ministries, a further extension of the relationship of bishop and deacon can be expressed in the deacon working with the team rector or incumbent who is there in the place of the bishop.

Collaborative sharing in the vocation to be ambassadors for Christ leads to the charge, 'You are to proclaim the gospel in word and deed as agents of God's purposes of love for all his people.' The use of the word 'proclaim' opens up wide possibilities in the catechetical ministry of the deacon: the dictionary definitions include 'publish abroad'. As described here it embraces anything that enables God's love for all his people to be made manifest, but the Church of England has tended to equate it with preaching, whereas the Methodist Church makes a distinction between preaching and non-preaching deacons. The assumption that deacons preach appears to be based on the assumption that most deacons will be ordained priest in due course and that diaconal ministry is principally training for the priestly ministry. However, with the re-emergence of the diaconate as a distinctive vocation, the use of 'proclaim' in the ordination service opens up new possibilities for exploration of a wider diaconal ministry of proclamation freed from a preaching emphasis.

In the Diocese of Salisbury our discussions led us to the conclusion that whilst regular preaching during the principal Sunday services is not necessarily integral to the ministry of deacons, particularly where the ministry of Readers is strong, nevertheless deacons may be called upon to preach at pastoral services and therefore it is appropriate that all deacons be trained to preach. The nature of diaconal ministry means that deacons may find themselves preaching at baptisms where they have prepared the candidate and family for the baptism, especially if the deacon's wider ministry was the catalyst for the person coming to church in the first place; similarly at marriages where the deacon has prepared the couple for marriage. The pastoral caring element of the ministry of deacons opens up the possibility of many funerals at which the deacon will preach as an integral part of the ongoing care offered to the deceased person prior to their death and their family and friends. Sermons and homilies preached on these occasions will be different to sermons preached at a regular gathering of the worshipping congregation, and all deacons, whether future priests or not, need to be able to put the word of God in dialogue with the particular pastoral occasion, and proclaim the word of God in that situation. This is part of the process of helping people over the threshold into church.

Other situations where deacons are called to proclaim the gospel in words could include family services, particularly if the deacon is also active in the local school during the week and thus can help people over the threshold between school and church; and nursing home services where a few appropriate words and a known hymn can go a very long way in proclaiming the gospel to the elderly and sick. It is not just about gaining converts but the more demanding and long-term work of what William Abraham describes as 'primary initiation into the kingdom of God'.[14] In all these situations there is a need for more than knowledge of Scripture, important as that is; there is also the need for knowledge of the hearers and discernment of how God is speaking to them at this time. This knowledge is gained through the deacon's life in the world and in church, observing and getting to know the people and the places encountered there. Added to this is skill in preparing a homily that puts word and life in dialogue. This makes demands on us and Mother Mary Clare's wise counsel about spiritual direction is equally applicable to proclamation in pastoral ministry: 'The more a Christian keeps his own inner life God-orientated, the more he will realise that men have a desire to grow up in Christ and a real longing for God. So he will try to see what God is doing in others, keeping close to the Holy Spirit who is the true director of souls.'[15]

In order to be able to keep their inner lives God-orientated, deacons are charged by the bishop to seek nourishment from the Scriptures and to model their life upon them. This takes us back into the heart of the integration that is the hallmark of diaconal ministry – Scripture and life are in dialogue, the deacon's life is an articulation of Scripture that others can read. The biblical scholar Walter Brueggemann describes a priest but enunciates a principle that is equally true of the deacon: 'someone who is authorised in the community, who is recognised as having the capacity to bear and enact holiness among us, holiness that outruns our technical control and understanding'.[16] Brueggemann's reference to enacting holiness that outruns our understanding takes us back to the diaconal life as a holy life that asks questions. The vital link, articulated in the ordinal, is the seeking nourishment in, and modelling life upon, the Scriptures. The deacon does this himself or herself, and also leads others in reflection upon the Scriptures. There is always a public element to the deacon's engagement with Scripture, unlike personal

Bible study which all Christians can do and which should be part of the deacon's own discipline. The charge to reflect on Scripture with God's people assumes a good grounding in Scripture and theology that is part of the training of a deacon. It opens up many possibilities: leading a small Bible study group or an inquirers' group, sitting in someone's living room and looking together at a Bible passage, or speaking a few well-chosen words in the context of a bedside communion in a hospital. And the reason for reflecting on Scripture in this way? It is so that the whole church may be equipped to live out the gospel in the world. Indeed, if the deacon does not lead people in reflection that inspires and enables them to live the gospel in the world, the deacon's own ministry in the world will suffer because he or she will be doing it all on behalf of people who see no need to be engaged for themselves. The danger of separating ministry in the world from ministry in the church is that people in church can abdicate their responsibility to the deacon. However, if the deacon who is known to be actively engaged in ministry in the world is the same person who reflects with the people of God on God's word and their own vocation to serve God, who catechizes and leads them by example in living the gospel wherever they are, then there can be no excuse for anyone to drive a wedge between seeking nourishment in Scripture and getting deeply involved in the world: there is no option of it being 'either/or' since the deacon embodies the complementarity. This is what Bishop Tom Ray was driving at when he spoke of deacons not doing our work for us but revealing and shining a light on the servant ministry that is already embedded in our lives. He spoke of the diaconate as a clear window through which to see that ordered ministry is not territorial but instead reveals to us a dimension of the depth of meaning of our own baptism.[17]

The final part of the Bishop's charge that has bearing on catechetical ministry is the charge to be 'faithful in prayer, expectant and watchful for the signs of God's presence, as he reveals his kingdom among us'. Here the integration is between prayer, expectant waiting, and revealing the signs of God's presence. Again this bridges the tempting divide between private and public, between prayer on the one hand and the ability to read the signs of the times. In the middle of this there is the phrase, 'expectant and watchful'. So much waiting is far from watchful but is oblivious of what is going on around, or is waiting in a hopeless way. The deacon, called to expectant and watchful looking for the signs of God's presence, looks perceptively and proclaims the truth that God is present, whether or not that appears obvious to others at the particular moment. Indeed, helping others to look is a catechetical ministry. This requires an immersion in God's word and in prayer that enables the deacon to observe, like a watchman, the signs that God is on the move. This is a gift to the world where so many people feel abandoned not only by God but also by the people they thought they could trust, or by the system that was supposed to meet their needs. To be able to sit with someone for whom hope is a lost commodity and to have the active patience rooted in God, with the ability to detect the presence of God that encourages another person to begin to hope, is a rich blessing we can offer. Diaconal ministry includes making hope visible, not as abstract hope but as hope that is grounded in God, the fruit of a vibrant prayer life, and capable of interpretation and revelation in the world. In Scripture we see Jeremiah struggling with his own loss of hope, his own sense of being tricked or abandoned by God, but then able to proclaim the presence and word of God to the people because he had done his own honest, and at times bitter, wrestling with God behind the scenes.

Because diaconal ministry is so deeply incarnational, engaged with our world in all its majesty and muddle, the proclamation of deacons needs to pay attention to the context in which it is made. We read of Jesus being brought up in a particular place at a particular time, travelling from place to place in a particular geographical area ruled by a particular power. Nazareth was different from Jerusalem, Galilee from Jericho. Life is lived in its particularity. Unless we acknowledge this, our catechetical ministry will pass people by or be misunderstood. Life is different in Salisbury and Sri Lanka, in Kansas and Khartoum. In *A Christian Theology of Place* John Inge explores the significance of place and draws out the important point for deacons that places develop their own story as a result of human experience in them.[18] Our catechism and our lives need to take account of the stories of place as we are open to encounter God for ourselves in the place where we are set. Kathleen Norris had to re-establish herself in the windswept and isolated town in Kansas that was so different to the city to which she had become accustomed, and to learn to encounter God there. Belden Lane had to accommodate himself to the confined and unaesthetic nursing home room that became his mother's home for the last part of her life. This can be called inhabiting a place:

> To *inhabit* a place is to dwell there in a practised way, in a way which relies upon certain regular, trusted, habits of behaviour. . . . We take it for granted that the way we live in a place is a matter of individual choice . . . We have largely lost the sense that our capacity to live well in a place might depend upon our ability to relate to neighbours (especially neighbours with a different lifestyle) on the basis of shared habits of behaviour. . . . In fact, no real public life is possible except among people who are engaged in the project of inhabiting a place.[19]

Deacons should be setting an example to the church of inhabiting the neighbourhood, recognizing this influence of place and context and able to adapt the method of proclamation so that the church can live out the gospel in the particular corner of the world in which it is located. Diaconal ministry in the inner city is both the same as and very different to diaconal ministry in a deeply rural area or a busy general hospital: the gospel and basic human needs are the same, but the task of the deacon is to interpret both so that the gospel can be proclaimed with power and grace. So a basic question for deacons is, 'How do I inhabit my neighbourhood?' Only if we inhabit can we catechize well, because only then will we, like George Herbert, be able to frame the questions that help people to find the answers.

PART 3

THE GROUNDWORK OF DIACONAL MINISTRY

7

Pray

Being people of prayer

Michael Ramsey's classic definition of priestly prayer, 'being before God with the people on your heart',[1] has stood the test of time. It is as true for deacons as it is for priests, and points to the twofold nature of prayer for the minister. We are not alone when we pray – quite apart from the whole company of heaven, of whose praying and praising presence we remind ourselves in every Eucharist, as deacons we come before God with others on our heart: other people with whose care we have been entrusted.

As deacons we are charged with being faithful in prayer, expectant and watchful for signs of God's presence, as he reveals his kingdom among us.[2] Although the 1550 Ordinal for the Ordering of Deacons (printed in the 1662 Book of Common Prayer) does not refer to prayer when describing the calling and ministry of a deacon, it is hinted at in phrases like 'a ready will to observe all spiritual Discipline'. The *Alternative Service Book* and the current draft Ordinal are less ambiguous: prayer is part of the vocation of the deacon. From the Orthodox tradition comes the question whether deacons, because they perhaps more than any other order are called to minister to spiritually hungry people, need more spiritual preparation, theological and pastoral training than that expected for other clergy.[3] Within this spiritual preparation is stability in prayer. The 'more than' component does not arise for Anglicans given that all clergy are deacons, but the point is well made and reinforces the importance of being called to this ministry by the Church which recognises one's preparedness, rather than taking it upon oneself.

Part of ministerial formation that should take place during training is the development of a disciplined personal prayer life that will stand the demands of ordained ministry and is in place at ordination, because all future ministry will founder if the deacon cannot or does not pray. In the ordination service the bishop asks about the deacons' intention to be diligent in prayer, reading Scripture and all studies that will deepen their faith and fit them to uphold the truth of the gospel against error. A further question is whether, in the strength of the Holy Spirit, they will continually stir up the gift of God that is in them. The reason for this is that they may grow stronger and more mature in their ministry, and that the lives of both deacon and those they serve should be transformed by the word of God. These are weighty but vital commitments that require action from us, an energetic and hungry hankering after the work of the Holy Spirit in our lives, and prayer is central to this deepening and maturing. A pattern of prayer that was adequate before ordination may not be adequate after ordination and diaconal ministry will show up the strengths or weaknesses of our prayer life. There has to be a scaffolding or framework of prayer in place that can bear the weight to be placed upon it, and regular testing with the assistance of a spiritual director of how it is holding up. If we are honest, most of us find prayer does not always come naturally, so discipline is needed.

Research shows[4] that congregations want their ministers to pray for them, and those to be ordained deacon promise, with God's help, to be diligent in prayer. I remember, just prior to my own ordination when faced with the enormity of what I was committing myself to, realizing just how grateful I was for those few words, 'With the help of God, I will', which would be part of my answer to the bishop about my commitment to prayer and all the other things I was saying yes to. Prayer, indeed all ministry, is with the help of God. But since we pray differently and are in different circumstances we are responsible for our own discipline of prayer. This may not be identical for all of us but we are all explicitly committed to prayer.[5] This is not an arbitrary requirement, it is a recognition of the demands that public ministry, let alone our family's needs, places upon us, and it is realistic about the ability we all have to find something much more urgent to do than to pray. It reflects Forbes Robinson's insight over a century ago: 'Your influence, your life, your all, depends on prayer.'[6] It also reflects the fact that prayer is a natural expression of who we are; hence Michael Mayne's reflection after a lifetime of ordained ministry:

Prayer is not an escape from life, a few minutes cut out of life, but a regular, disciplined reminder that all life is lived in God's presence, a marvelling at God's love as that is shown in Christ, a thankful responding to that transcendent reality by whom we are held in being.

Prayer, then, is not primarily something I do in order to achieve something, but something I do because this is the sort of creature I am called to be: one who has an intuitive sense of the transcendent, a muffled but persistent sense of the presence of the holy.[7]

Prayer is something we do: we set aside specific time for prayer and need to learn to become masters not servants of time. We may have a place to which we go to pray – whether a church, or a corner of a room, or a particular chair – since this helps to focus the mind. But it is also true that prayer pervades all of life, it cannot be reduced to what we do at particular times. In the eighteenth century Jean de Caussade spoke and wrote of 'the sacrament of the present moment' in which we can find God in the midst of life. The truth is that we need both discipline and freedom, prayer as act and prayer as ethos. So, while it may be true that we pray when we are out and about in our daily lives, when we see a beautiful sunset or meet a situation of great need, there is a danger that the *ad hoc* aspect of this approach puts our prayer life at the mercy of what happens to us in daily life. If there is no beautiful sunset or situation of need, do we pray? Equally, if we only pray when at a particular time and place, are we in danger of legalism or attributing false sanctity to the time of day or the place chosen? Fairly regularly I meet students whose prayer life consists almost entirely of one or the other approach, and part of training is to encourage a broadening in prayer. It is exciting when this happens and a previously unfamiliar, even feared, way of prayer becomes life-giving and another part of the tool bag of spiritual disciplines that underlie the emerging ministry. This is in line with St Isaac of Syria's advice not to abandon fixed forms of prayer but not to reduce prayer to them: 'Do not reduce your prayer to words, make the totality of your life a prayer to God.' Or, even more directly, holding the balance Bishop Hugh Montefiore referred to: 'Holiness means living within the divine perspective. It comes from attention to God – on your knees in prayer; and it comes from obedience to God – on your feet in action.'[8]

There is another creative tension, that of praying alone and praying with others. Again it is a both/and situation; as deacons we are
public people with public responsibilities, and people will look to
us for an example in prayer. So we need to be praying with others,
but we also need to pray alone since there are some things that need
the time and space that public prayer cannot give – from our own
intercessions for other people to contemplation, from meditation on
God's word at our own pace to wrestling with God when we have a
particular issue that will not resolve lightly.

Being before God in the midst of a demanding ministry

There are many helpful books on prayer and this chapter does
not duplicate them but focuses on the deacon at prayer.[9] What is
prayer for deacons who are charged with the particular responsibilities that ordination lays upon us, and which we cannot fulfil in our
own strength? For many people around the world, Mother Teresa
exemplified diaconal ministry. Her motivation was love for God
that could not ignore the needs of some of the most outcast people
in society. She was in a public role but never abandoned her own
practical ministry and was committed to her monastic discipline of
prayer, with time set aside in a day that could be filled to the last
second with essential, practical caring. If ever a Christian could be
said to be too busy to pray it was Mother Teresa, yet she encouraged
others to pray by example and by her words: 'Love to pray – feel
the need to pray often during the day and take the trouble to pray.
If you want to pray better, you must pray more. Prayer enlarges the
heart until it is capable of containing God's gift of himself. Ask and
seek and your heart will grow big enough to receive him and keep
him as your own.'[10]
Having our heart enlarged until it is capable of containing God's
gift of himself shifts the emphasis from the task that we do, for
which we pray, onto the person that we are before God. Always in
prayer there is a formative aspect: the person who rises from prayer
to fulfil the ministry to which he or she is called is in some way different from the person who knelt to pray. It may be that we have
a new perspective on what we are praying for, or – more likely but
perhaps less noticeable to us – we may ourselves be changed in the

way we live. It was regular prayer that enabled Mother Teresa to sustain the demanding schedule that ministry placed upon her and it was prayer that sustained her predecessors in the nineteenth century where the revival in regular weekday celebration of the Eucharist in the Church of England was due, in large part, to the needs of the nuns working in inner-city slums. The Methodist Church in England reopened its Methodist Diaconal Order in 1986 and all deacons belong to it, accepting the discipline that includes commitment to prayer and mutual support to sustain them in the isolation of much of their work. The commitment to set time aside for prayer on a regular basis is formative in itself as our priorities are daily reordered.

This need to have a prayer pattern in place that will sustain us, whatever is thrown at us, was recognized by Baron von Hugel when he wrote to one of the people who looked to him for spiritual guidance, using words that could be written for and of deacons whose ministry faces them with illness, crisis and death:

> I want to prepare you, to organise you for life, for illness, for crisis, and death. . . . Live all you can – as complete and full a life as you can find – do as much as you can for others. Read, work, enjoy – love and help as many souls – do all this. Yes – but remember: Be alone, be remote, be away from the world, be desolate. Then you will be near God.[11]

We have to find this time. It won't find itself.

Brother Lawrence, the kitchen-hand monk, tells of his experience in the monastic kitchens. His insights, now published as *The Practice of the Presence of God*, help us to translate the idea that we can pray at any time into the practice of prayer. We need to remember that he was a monk, and thus his prayer life was shaped through the monastic commitment to regular times of prayer. This underlying discipline bore fruit in the chaos of the kitchen just before meal time: 'The time of business does not with me differ from the time of prayer; and in the noise and clatter of my kitchen, while several persons are at the same time calling for different things, I possess God in as great tranquillity as if I were on my knees at the Blessed Sacrament.'[12] The shortcut we seek is the tranquillity in the kitchen (whatever that is in our diaconal ministry) without the foundation of the 'time of prayer' to which Brother Lawrence refers. We are not all monastics and do not have the luxury or the burden, depending upon how we see it, of being required to pray at certain times throughout the day. Yet time and again we see the stress that is rightly laid upon prayer. But in the story of Martha and Mary (Luke 10.38–42) the traditional assumption, that Mary got it right by sitting at Jesus' feet whilst Martha got it wrong because she was busy in the kitchen, reflects the old view that the monastic contemplative vocation was better than the lay vocation to life in the world. It is time that was discredited. If we look closely at what Jesus said to Martha he does not comment upon the relative value of being active or contemplative, but upon the fact that she is distracted whilst Mary is focused. Presumably he was very grateful that Martha was cooking in the kitchen: after all, he had come for a meal and there were no takeaways then! The interpretative tradition that we inherit is not helpful and we lose the point about distraction. We can be just as distracted sitting in silence as we can be in the kitchen since we may bring inner chaos to the sitting still; the substance of Martha's complaint to Jesus points us to the source of her distraction, she felt uncared for by Jesus and ignored by Mary.

Michael Ramsey looked for priests to be a deep reservoir from which water can flow steadily, not just a conduit or canal. That is perhaps one difference between the ministry of the deacon and the ministry of lay people: the deacon amongst other things is an innovator, a catalyst, a resource person, a pace-setter in ministry. To be this, our imaginations are stretched, our boundaries are pushed back and our vision clarified by God as we pray. For this there has to be space; as Jeremy Taylor put it, 'There should be in the soul halls of space, avenues of leisure and high porticos of silence, where God waits.'[13] Then God can meet with us to sustain and nurture us as people who develop the ministry in which we and others are engaged. Ramsey was realistic about the demands that ministry places upon us in the long term, about how easy it is to lose the spark that ignites, the vision of Christ that inspires, and to be caught up in the 'hazards of monotony, professionalism, habit, staleness, tiredness and perfunctoriness'. His remedies for this were: 'the sense of wonder in worship, the acceptance of unsought humiliations as drawing close to the suffering and joy of Christ, and being open to Christ in other people, and to the rekindling effect of his truth and love evident in their lives'.[14]

Although prayer is not mentioned as such, wonder in worship, acceptance of humiliations and the rekindling effect of truth and love are all the fruit of prayer which is opening ourselves to God. They take us beyond where we thought we could go when routine is trapping us or we are content with mere survival. Prayer is not just about the third parties for whom we pray, it is also always about us before God. Thus there is always another dynamic when we pray about situations encountered in ministry: in prayer God is also working in us as well as through our diaconal ministry. As John Udris puts it:

> The greatest confirmation that I am where I should be is whether or not I am being challenged and changed. . . . [M]inistry constantly prises me out – out of my comfort zones, out of myself. It will not allow me to stay put, it stretches me and takes me to places I would not otherwise go. . . . I suggest that the most persuasive proof of any authentic call of God lies in the conversion it always calls forth.[15]

The Rule of Benedict may be 1500 years old, but it is remarkably contemporary even though cultures have changed. In the following extract Benedict is writing, and Joan Chittister commenting, on the monastic practice of eating in silence while listening to a reading.

> 'Let there be complete silence. No whispering, no speaking – only the reader's voice should be heard there. The members should by turn serve one another's needs as they eat and drink, so that no one need ask for anything.' (Rule of Benedict 38) In the course of the meal, the monastics are to concentrate on two things: the words of the reading and the needs of their neighbours. It is an astounding demonstration of the nature of the entire Christian life frozen in a single frame. We are to listen intently for the Word of God and be aware of those around us at the same time. Either one without the other is an incomplete Christianity.[16]

The details may be different for us since few of us are in a position to follow this practice (although it may not be so different from listening to tapes while driving), but the principle is helpful. In particular, it points to the integration of prayer and listening for God with awareness of the situations around us in which we live and serve. We are challenged to listen intently for the Word of God and be aware of those around us at the same time. And if we can't do this at meal times because family life is not monastic, the question is when do we find the time to listen, to be formed by what we read and hear? What do we read? Does it draw us closer to God and equip us for our ministry? Do we make time to meditate? To pray? To notice the needs of those around us?

Benedict is leading us towards the insight that meditation is not really about spending time having beautiful thoughts, but about building up a Christian memory so that we have the resources to fulfil our ministry in the world. It is only when we know God and God's ways with the world, a knowledge gained in part through prayer and study, that we have resources to draw on when things go wrong. Much diaconal ministry is about things that have gone wrong – sickness, unemployment, poverty, suffering, death, marginalization – and so deacons need to be well resourced through prayer and study to interpret to others what God is doing and to sustain themselves. This involves study of Scripture and theology and the Christian tradition. It may include study of the world, its institutions and its ways of ordering its life. When we are praying for or with people for whom things have gone wrong, the ability to suspend judgement, to postpone conclusions, may be helpful, along with immersion in the Psalms since the Psalmists invite us to join them as they and we wrestle with problems before God rather than push to hasty conclusions. Eventually we will move on, like the Psalmists, to examine the memory of the tradition and God's ways in the past – praying ourselves round to taking a longer perspective on current woes. Some questions need to wait until things are less volatile and there is the emotional stability to allow the questions to be explored. Our diaconal ministry involves us in helping to hold people during the period when it is too early to examine questions in any depth. Only maturity expressed in a stable prayer life – a disciplined prayer life that holds us to keep praying, either on our own or in the liturgical worship of the church – will enable us to fulfil our diaconal ministry to those in need. And so we turn to the second half of Michael Ramsey's saying, having others on our heart when we pray.

Being before God for others

As deacons, we cannot keep prayer in a vacuum because communion with God brings with it communion with others – we worship
a Trinitarian God who, in Christ, has shared our life and drawn us
to share God's life. 'The door of prayer towards heaven, towards
the heart of God, is always a door of love into the world of human
needs.'[17] These words of Michael Ramsey reflect his own experience
of praying for the people with whose care he had been entrusted.
Prayer involves other people: praying for them, bringing their joys
and sorrows to God, teaching and leading them in prayer themselves. Sean Connolly draws attention to Ramsey's insight that

> the original meaning of the Greek word which we translate as
> 'intercession' was not 'to make petition' or to pray or speak for,
> as we tend to think. Rather it was a notion of presence. It meant
> encountering someone on behalf of, or in relation to, others. . . .
> What is presented here, according to Ramsey, is a theology of
> being rather than doing. Christ is for us. By virtue of our ordina-
> tion, we priests are now for others. We share in this intercessory
> ministry of Christ the head.[18]

Connolly then notes that whilst prayer is seen to be the job of the
minister this is a misinterpretation of the truth. Instead, 'our job is
to be a sign of the prayerfulness of all the faithful. Prayer – at least
at times – has been delegated by the people to the priest, when in
reality it is the priest who should be helping the people to pray themselves.'[19] Part of the catechetical ministry of the deacon is to help
people to pray, teaching not only by word but by helping those who
are running into problems in their own prayer. This may involve
praying with them, either individually or in a small group, thus
teaching by example, or it may involve a short course on prayer. For
most people, prayer is effectively intercession and perhaps praise,
both of which are good but not the whole story, and broadening
people's horizons in prayer is part of this helping with prayer. Since
people pray differently, deacons should be equipped to help people
to pray in ways that are appropriate for them and should be able
to recognize the signs that someone could be shown more helpful
ways to pray. To do this we will find ourselves experimenting with

different ways to pray since this is integral to being before God for others. In addition, we should not neglect the people, often the elderly, who are more mature in prayer than others, to whom we can turn for encouragement and support, or with prayer requests that are not confidential. Thus in one church we matched elderly 'prayers' with Sunday School classes, asking them to be aunt or uncle to that class and to pray for them. In return the children offered them their love, their friendship and their creative offerings. The children never guessed the extent of the prayer for them, but the benefit to both young and old was tangible and the elderly were encouraged to take new responsibility in prayer.

Prayer for others cannot be divorced from pastoral care. Michael Ramsey articulates this seamless weaving of prayer and care, quoting Gregory the Great's letter in 598 to Eulogius, the Bishop of Alexandria: 'Intercession lies at the heart of Christianity, for an act of kindness must also be an act of prayer, and prayer must serve where practical acts cannot be achieved. As in these words of Gregory the Great "your prayers are at work where you are not; your holy works are evident where you are".'[20] In fulfilling this responsibility, Jeremy Taylor cast a wide net in prayer, looking to the healing of the world as well as local needs, and implying that we are willing to be part of the answer to our own prayers for the world's healing. In his context of the violence of the Civil War, that was a demanding and perhaps dangerous thing to do. 'Pray much and very fervently for all your parishioners, and all men that belong to you, and all that belong to God . . . ever remembering, that you are by God appointed as ministers of prayer, and the ministers of good things, to pray for all the world, and to heal all the world, as far as you are able.'[21]

Because prayer is integral to diaconal ministry, not an add-on, living our prayer is as much a part of praying as voicing it. And if we do pray for all the world, as Jeremy Taylor advocates, we will find ourselves being drawn into engagement with world issues as part of diaconal ministry. Environmental issues, political issues, business ethics, industrial relations, relief work across the world: all belong in our prayers and our service. Praying with the newspapers or the TV news is a way of keeping abreast of these matters, practising – as Lawrence practised in his kitchen – the presence of God as we read and listen to stories from around the world, refusing to ignore the harrowing or the hilarious that may need to be prayed about because it affects someone's life. Another approach is to cut out, and keep as reminders to pray, the pictures that challenge us with matters too big for words. Children have pictures on their walls at school, perhaps deacons should have pictures in their study to stir them to pray. We are intercessors for the world, sharing the servant ministry of Jesus Christ who blended prayer and compassionate action seamlessly.

Intercession for others is central to diaconal prayer, along with more colloquial prayer that ponders and probes the situations we encounter, seeking perspective on them. But there is a further strand to prayer and Desmond Tutu has observed that if governments knew the dangers of apophatic prayer (prayer that opens us to the mystery of God rather than to what can be known of God) they would ban it immediately. He says that no threat is as dangerous as the power of a people radically set free from the value structures of their world.[22] If Tutu is right, then diaconal ministry in the world can be sustained not just by intercession for the needs we encounter but by this less wordy way of prayer in which we are drawn into the mystery of God. As Thomas Merton put it, 'Without contemplation and interior prayer the church cannot fulfil her mission to transform and save mankind. Without contemplation, she will be reduced to being the servant of cynical and worldly powers, no matter how hard her faithful may protest that they are fighting for the Kingdom of God.'[23] Or, as Kenneth Leech writes from the context of inner London, 'It is the mystical element which gives warmth, humanity and tolerance, and without which religions can grow hard, inflexible and cruel. It is the mystical element which integrates theology, action and prayer.'[24] Elsewhere Leech puts this in theological terms that point to God's radical taking of human flesh in a broken world: 'Prayer then is the interiorising of the Incarnation. The Word is to become enfleshed in me. Bethlehem is here. So Christmas Day is to become all days, and the adoration of Emmanuel, God with us, must be a daily and continuous event.'[25]

That is a salutary challenge when prayer is in danger of becoming functional, driven by the needs we encounter, a shopping list of urgent requests. At such times, and there will be many such times, we are asked to slow down and get things in perspective, to adore God who has come among us. We are not to neglect the needs of the world, for they are part of our responsibility as deacons, but neither are we to neglect the bigger theological picture into which our ministry is set and which prayer keeps in our sights. That is a diaconal way of praying.

8

Love

Being lovers

The authentic cadence was discovered late
Which ends those only strains that I approve,
And other science all gone out of date
And minor sweetness scarce made mention of:
I have found the dominant of my range and state –
Love, O my God, to call Thee Love and Love.[1]

In these words we are given an early glimpse of the 'dominant'
in Gerard Manley Hopkins's life: Love of God who is Love. In
expressing this, he stood in a long Christian tradition. Thus Thomas
Traherne wrote that we 'are as prone to love as the sun is to shine'.[2]
For Teresa of Avila the important thing was not to think much but
to love much and so she taught her nuns to do whatever aroused
them to love, saying that love consists not in the extent of our
happiness but in the firmness of our determination to try to please
God in everything. Teresa's friend John of the Cross, who encountered much lack of love from the Church, which imprisoned him for
long periods, taught that where there is no love we must put love in
in order that we might draw love out. There is an act of determined
love in diaconal ministry that is directed to God and seeks to see and
serve God in and through whomever and whatever we meet.

Love draws its nature from God's love which is multi-faceted and
constantly tends to glorious excess. God is love and the love of the
Trinity is well described as a dance of love that is vibrant, outgoing,
relational and inclusive. Because God is Trinity, love overflows, and
in and through the incarnate and ascended Second Person of the

Trinity we humans are caught up in God's love. Thus we do not have to manufacture love of our own, but live into and share the love of God: 'we love, because he first loved us' (1 John 4.19). Kenneth Leech puts this quite starkly when he writes in words that reflect the Orthodox Church's theological emphasis:

> The whole notion of an 'inner life' is a post-Reformation develop-ment. Today, at least in evangelical circles, we talk about 'bringing Jesus into my life' whereas the New Testament speaks of bringing us into Christ's life. The entire thrust of the New Testament is the new creation, the new humanity in Christ, the building up of the body of Christ, the coming to the fullness of God.[3]

In this building up of the body of Christ, deacons are caught up in the love of God. Brought into Christ's life, we are more than just conduits of God's love, we put our own imprint on it, so that in us people encounter not God's raw love but God's love expressed in us. Obviously this brings responsibilities, but it also opens up enormous creative diversity – since we are all so different there are many dif-ferent expressions of God's love in diaconal ministry. That is part of the wonder of God's creativity. Love, however, is costly since it takes its lead from the love of Jesus Christ, and we should not overlook the fact that we are called to give ourselves away, that all ministry is essentially sacrificial and demanding. Bishop John Taylor taught:

> For those created in the divine image it follows that real human life is likewise about giving ourselves away. Real human life necessitates self-emptying, self-giving, self-limiting in order to be freely available. Indeed, there can be no chauvinism here for this is the pattern of the whole creation and of all creaturely life. The incarnation is typical of God, always and everywhere. Incarna-tion supplies the essential clue apart from which we might not see how the cosmos holds together. In other words, there is a univer-sal principle of life-through-death, of individual self-immolation in the interests of a larger claim, which is at variance with the universal principle of self-preservation.[4]

That is true of all ministry but John Wesley argued that those entrusted with the care of others are called to show still greater love than what he calls 'ordinary Christians'. Here he is addressing the clergy about their vocation, their love for God and others, setting before them a challenge in their discipleship beyond that of all the baptized: 'As to his *Affections*. Ought not a *Steward of the Mysteries of GOD*, a Shepherd of the Souls for whom *Christ* died, to be endued with an eminent Measure of Love to GOD and Love to all his Brethren? A Love the same in Kind, but in Degree far beyond that of ordinary Christians?'[5]

Because God is love, God is both aware of and attentive to our needs. Cardinal Basil Hume wrote of two needs, to worship and to be saved. God became man to enable us to worship and to heal our wounds.[6] Diaconal ministry, which draws its motivation from God's incarnational love in Jesus Christ, understands the need to worship and the need to be saved, and is directed towards both ends. That is the genius of the blend of the liturgical and pastoral in the ministry of the deacon as it expresses the wholeness of God's love for us. Whereas the world is always trying to make our wants into needs – advertising expresses this so blatantly – God in his love is in the business of turning our needs into wants. As we open ourselves to God we find that not only do we need to worship, but also we want to worship, not only do we need to be healed but also we want to be healed – Jesus often questioned people about what they wanted even when the need appeared obvious: did the blind man really want to see? Did the lame men really want to walk (Luke 18.41; John 5.6)? Were they ready to take the responsibility for having their needs met and their lives thus turned around? to live as healed and whole people? Here we can see the third strand of diaconal ministry coming in – the catechetical strand which, amongst other things, helps people to understand the life they are embracing when they respond to God's love. And this requires inner work within the deacon. Then we can rise to the challenge given to deacons in Sweden:

> Meet people tenderly and with respect,
> together with them
> seek the way God wills,
> and let it be your endeavour
> to let faith, doctrine and life become one.[7]

God's love, whilst available to all and all-embracing, is never just in the abstract or in theory. William Blake's pithy and provocative remark that 'If you would be good you must do it in minute particulars'[8] is echoed by Hans Küng: 'Jesus, however, is not interested in universal, theoretical or poetical love. . . . it is a love, not of man in general, of someone remote, with whom we are not personally involved, but quite concretely love of one's immediate neighbour. . . . *anyone who wants me here and now.*'[9]

Jesus' life was a constant series of interruptions by people who wanted him 'here and now' and he responded to them whilst also safeguarding time away from their demands. Most of us prefer some semblance of order to our day, and deacons who can live peacefully with demands at all times are a particular gift to people in need. Cultivating the ability to be centred whilst also available to others is part of diaconal formation and it may take working at, whether our natural inclination is to be so centred that we cannot be disturbed or so available that we cannot be focused. One of the attributes selectors look for in candidates for ordination is sufficient maturity and stability to show that they are able to sustain the demanding role of a minister and to face change and pressure in a flexible and balanced way. Candidates should be people of integrity.[10] Integrity implies a wholeness and consistency in our being so that we can handle pressure and change without fraying at the edges. For this some boundaries are essential if families are not to be resentful of the amount of time spent on the job, rather than with them. It is easy for deacons to impose unrealistic expectations on themselves or to be trapped by the sometimes unreasonable expectations of others, including the church. Jesus' summary of the law involves loving God and loving our neighbour as we love ourselves. We cannot have one without the other two, and love for God that excludes love for our families and for ourselves is suspect love.

The love of God

The love of God is the dominant in our lives and evokes a response in us. Most people in training for ordination speak of a sense of awe and wonder that God has called them to this, and express a deep love of God in their conduct, worship and approach to their studies.

There can be no doubt that love for God motivates them, and the excitement of beginning training, the tenacity in the tougher times, and the joy at ordination are all evidence of this loving response to God's love. But there are times in ministry when it is harder for the long haul, when love is tested and loving duty needs to kick in, and in those times Simon Patrick's words to his clergy while he was Bishop of Ely in the 1690s are pertinent. Here his reminder of their vocation to love God includes the reminder of the words spoken by the bishop at their ordination and the effectual prayer thus constituted: God's love sustains us.

> And above all things, you must labour to possess your hearts with a spirit of love to God, whose servants you are, and who employs you in the most glorious work in the world. . . . [Recalling the words spoken at their ordination: 'Receive the Holy Ghost for the office and work of a priest in the church of God':] These were not empty words, nor mere lofty expressions without any power in them; but an effectual prayer for the Holy Spirit of grace which was then conferred upon you: and should mightily move you to serve the church of Christ in the love of the Spirit. . . . For if we preserve this flame in our hearts, it will make us cheerful as well as diligent, restless and unwearied in the work of the Lord. Nothing can carry us through it like this, and render it so easy and sweet to us, as to think we are serving our good God in that which he loves and delights to have done; and to feel that everything we do proceeds from love to him and to his service.[11]

Our love to God, which we can rightly labour to possess in our hearts, is part of a reciprocal relationship of love: ordination is not just about the ministry to which we are called, it is about the love and indwelling of God. Patrick's final sentence in this extract summarizes the virtuous circle of love of a God whose service is perfect freedom, in which deacons are caught up.

Paul reminds us that 'Love is patient and kind' (1 Corinthians 13.4); patient with others and with ourselves, but also with God when we are impatient for things to change. Diaconal ministry brings us up against situations where the patience of love is tested, and our formation involves maturing in patience. Otherwise we will try to force situations to premature conclusions and thus do damage. The following extract is a stark reminder of the discipline involved in our own patient maturing in the love of God in the context of ordained ministry. In summary, the letter from which this is an extract says that if our habits, not just our individual acts, are godly then when situations arise that stretch us beyond our known capacities we can rely on the formational work that has gone on in us to bear its own good fruit. If our love for God has not been expressed in willingness for formation that ingrains godly habits in us, then we will be out on a dangerous limb when we are placed under pressure. The author of the letter is Henry Dodwell, the recipient is someone soon to be ordained, the date is 1672 when there was great emphasis on holy living.

> You must . . . remember that the Calling you are undertaking will oblige you for your life . . . And for this end you must consider your qualifications themselves; whether they have appeared onely in *single Acts* or in *Habits*; or if in *Habits*, whether they be newly acquired or *strongly confirmed* and *rooted* by *custome*; for you cannot trust any other Habits for their duration for so long a time. Beside, you must consider whether your Temper be *fickle* or stable: if it be fickle, you can trust no Habits themselves longer than you can persevere in the same humour, or till they may decay gradually according to the method of their acquisition. . . . Nor would I have you think I herein make your *future* hopes of the grace of God a *Cypher*, in requiring you to foresee all future difficulties, and to measure them by proportion to your *present strengths*; so you see I do not deny the necessitie of the grace of God for bringing you to this excellent frame of Spirit I have hitherto been describing.[12]

This is sobering and, although we can say that it is a child of its time, it is essentially about building a Christian character with God's grace, as opposed to seeing formation just as the constant making of individual decisions. As such it is a salutary counterbalance to the contemporary emphasis (particularly in some worship songs) on love for God as an emotion or feeling within ourselves that has no other point of reference, and no formative impact on the way we live. If we love God our lives, not just our emotions, will express this. There is a basic link between our love for God and our manner of life and our attitudes: love leads us to discipline. Each morning during term time at 8.00 the boys' and girls' choirs at Salisbury Cathedral rehearse, and sometimes the faint sound of vocal exercises can be heard in the Trinity Chapel where the early Eucharist is in progress. I am frequently struck when I hear the children by the complementarity of the two expressions of love for God – in prayer in the chapel and in rehearsal in the choir room.

One aspect of our love for God which tends to be overlooked is our care of God's creation. St Symeon the New Theologian, who lived a thousand years ago, had a very holistic understanding of the importance of the material creation and our care of it. God in his love did not only give us paradise but the earth, but we are charged with tilling and keeping it, the latter involving protection and preservation.[13] Creation is given for the common use and enjoyment of all people, and love for God and our neighbour therefore has to take account of the charge given to Adam and Eve in the Genesis stories to tend and keep God's creation. Since this responsibility is common to all humans, diaconal ministry must embrace it both in the work of the deacon and in the challenge that the deacon holds before the congregation. The Church has generally been weak in seeing this as part of ordained ministry. Environmental and ecological work are embraced in the charge given to deacons to be agents of God's love who bring to the Church the concerns and hopes of all God's people, serving the poor and weak, the oppressed and powerless. Deacons are to reach out into the forgotten corners of the world which is often where the environmental issues are evident. Earlier we referred to R. S. Thomas's 'belief dipped in manure'[14] which, if only read metaphorically rather than literally, misses the import of his words. He very clearly had the literal manure of Welsh hill farms in mind. What does belief dipped in manure look like? belief dipped in the stripping of the Amazon hardwood forests? belief dipped in Bhopal? belief dipped in the depletion of the ozone layer and global warming? These are issues of pastoral care and justice just as much as visiting the elderly and housebound. The Church was active in the crisis for farmers precipitated by the Foot and Mouth outbreak in 2001 and much of its work then was diaconal, expressing the type of engaged ministry at local level that Ben Quash referred to in Chapter 2. This hymn, written in response to the Methodist Church's search for a hymn that addressed the Church's concern for environmental and

ecological issues in the light of Foot and Mouth, looks at our relationship to creation and how our living may or may not be loving.

> When we gasp in awe and wonder
> At the world, O God, you made,
> Rolling hills and rugged outcrops,
> Crashing seas and woodland glade;
> When we grasp for words to thank you
> Yet we lack the fitting phrase,
> As we revel in creation
> Let enjoyment be our praise.
>
> When hearts break in grief and sadness
> At our reckless lack of care,
> Ravaged land, polluted cities,
> Cattle die, the poor despair;
> When we ache as bird-song ceases,
> Drought or floods cause suffering,
> Challenge us to new approaches,
> Healing, restoration bring.
>
> When your giving overwhelms us,
> Beauty shared as friend with friend,
> Make us wise and faithful stewards,
> Your creation ours to tend.
> When our living is not loving,
> Then, O God, disturb our ways,
> Through our joyful, faithful caring,
> Let creation ring with praise.[15]

Love for others

At the end of the ordination service, when the new deacons are
given their New Testaments, the bishop says to them, 'You have
been ordained deacon in the Church of God: take these scriptures
as a sign of the authority given you today to serve God's people in
love and teach them in his name'.[16] In that short sentence there is
a reminder that the authority of deacons is expressed in service of
God's people in love. It compresses into one phrase the authority

given to deacons: the deacon is essentially charged to love, following the example of Christ who washed people's feet. That Scripture[17] is read at ordinations, sometimes modelled as the bishop washes the deacons' feet, and exemplifies diaconal ministry. But it presupposes that we are also willing for Christ to wash our feet, since love is reciprocal.

In discussing the love that lies at the heart of diaconal ministry, Sven Erik Brodd argues that the fact that the Church is a community of love and *koinonia* is the only perspective from which deacons exercise a ministry of love together with the whole Church. He says that it is a nineteenth-century reversal of this idea that says that deacons' ministry is one of love because they take care of the poor.[18] Love is the fount, not just the expression, of diaconal ministry. Yet if we are honest, the vocation to love others is at times a joy and at times a trial. Because love for another means that we do not take authority for that person's life, we cannot expect or require people to do or be as we would like. Far from controlling others, love always frees them. We see Jesus watching people he loved (the rich young man, Judas) go, rather than constraining them against their will. When we are exasperated with someone, or dealing with someone whom we simply find it hard to like, Bishop Simon Patrick's reminder of the way to stir up our love can be helpful:

> Preserve therefore and keep alive in your hearts a spirit of love to the souls of men, especially to your parishioners. And there is no way to do this like to the consideration of what it cost to redeem them; no less than by the blood of the Son of God: who demonstrated thereby how precious they are in themselves, and how dear to him. Bestow a few thoughts upon this every day, and it will beget and continue in you the greatest kindness and tenderest compassion towards them: and that will move you to lay out yourselves with the utmost diligence in all the offices belonging to your function.[19]

This is creative love that sees and loves people (ourselves included) with God's compassion, and thus can love people out of mediocrity or complacency. Writing over three hundred years later, Sean Connolly expresses his vocation slightly differently but is hinting at the same thing, ministry that is born of love rather than professional duty. He ends with a telling reminder that loving others has to affect who we are, not just what we do.

> In many ways I do have an impossible job. The demands and expectation are sometimes simply too much. . . . But of course, just as with my prayer, my pastoral ministry is more than simply a job. Being a priest is ultimately what I am, and not what I do. My life, now, is to be lived for others. It is to be lived, not begrudgingly, but in love. And the challenge remains here too: the challenge to avoid becoming the pastoral professional; the challenge is to try to be someone for others.[20]

W. H. Vanstone describes God's love as giving evermore, with zeal and eager hands, venturing and expending all.[21] This was no abstract theological idea for Vanstone: his own ministry was deeply incarnational and grounded in the daily round of pastoral care in the parish, where love for others was given tangible form in so many remarkable and unremarkable ways. He said of the clergy who influenced his own ministry, 'It was not, I think, heroic self-denial that kept these men so faithful to pastoral ministry in their parish: it was the cool intellectual conviction that no other work or charge could possibly be more important than the work they did and the charge which they held.'[22] That is an attitude that is deeply loving but at the same time starkly practical and unsentimental. It is the attitude that enabled Belden Lane to sit with his mother through her long dying from cancer, facing into the restrictions he had to embrace in order to be alongside and truly present to her. His words echo the routineness of love and of much diaconal ministry as we love in the midst of tedium.

> I also realised that by this time my mother's dying had ceased to be 'exciting'. The initial intensity of the threat of death had given way to the dull ordinariness of a long and exhausting wait. I no longer teetered on the threshold between life and death, caught up in a tragic immediacy that gave meaning and pathos to life. I was no longer the bearer of profundity, a person made powerful by my proximity to pain. Instead I felt only the anguish, weariness and anger that often accompany protracted illness. . . .
> Of the three stages of growth in the spiritual life, the second

stage of illumination is the one most akin to the experience of the season of Ordinary Time in the Christian calendar. It requires the long and agonising patience of waiting. . . .

Difficult as it was, at first, to discern grace in the grotesque, it became even more difficult to discover grace in the prolonged redundancy of ordinariness. How could I adjust to life's untheatrical regularity when I'd been prepared for grand opera and dark tragedy. I could handle bad news. . . . But how would I deal with the uneventful and commonplace? It was the disconsolation of the ordinary that I found most difficult to accept. I needed a book about When Ordinary Things Happen to Average People. I needed a spirituality of the uneventful, of the low places in one's life that are neither deep nor exhilaratingly high.[23]

Our ministry as deacons puts us alongside people who are in Lane's situation of long-term responsibility for others. We may find ourselves in that position too. How can we or they experience the glance of God's love in the midst of the tediously ordinary? It is a truism, but amongst other things it is the ministry of presence, of being there – not necessarily with the answers but with consistency and encouragement – that can crack open the door and begin to make life hopeful, even if the immediate situation can never be right in our terms. Alongside this loving presence and loving prayer is loving catechetical ministry that helps people to pray with patience and perhaps protest so that they have some way to express their situation to God. Exposure to the Psalms, first for ourselves and then with others, can be very loving. Some of the more reckless psalms that we blanch to say in church are made for the hospital or prison. I remember one lady, newly diagnosed with virulent cancer, who wanted me to read a different protest psalm each time I visited, only later could she cope with the comfort of Psalm 23 which was too saccharine at first. Love for others can mean sparing them the platitudes and risking going out on a limb with them into marginal territory.

Knowing God's love ourselves

And so, finally, we turn to love for ourselves and our own knowledge of God's love. It comes as a surprise to many that God's call to us is not as harsh as we might have feared: God delights to work with our strengths, our passions and our interests. Frederick Beechner speaks of our vocation lying where our deep joy and the world's deep need meet,[24] but so often we think it lies simply where the need is, discounting joy as part of God's loving gift.

God's love is diaconal, wanting to help us over the threshold for ourselves, dealing with our resistances and fears, meeting our needs, drawing us to worship. George Herbert's words ring across the centuries telling of this experience:

> Love bade me welcome: yet my soul drew back,
> > Guilty of dust and sin.
> But quick-eyed Love, observing me grow slack
> > From my first entrance in,
> Drew nearer to me, sweetly questioning,
> > If I lacked anything.
>
> A guest, I answered, worthy to be here:
> > Love said, You shall be he.
> I the unkind, ungrateful? Ah my dear,
> > I cannot look on thee.
> Love took my hand, and smiling did reply,
> > Who made the eyes but I?
>
> Truth, Lord, but I have marred them: let my shame
> > Go where it doth deserve.
> And know you not, says Love, who bore the blame?
> > My dear, then I will serve.
> You must sit down, says Love, and taste my meat:
> > So I did sit and eat.[25]

God's love for us frees us to know ourselves, to mature as humans, knowing our strengths and weaknesses, what refreshes and stimulates us, enabling us to engage with life fully and enthusiastically. But it also faces us with being honest with ourselves, knowing where we can succumb to the mediocre or the wrong, when we risk burnout. Two Australian researchers have identified key areas that need to be nurtured if clergy burnout is to be prevented. These include developing a well-rounded life, treating families very carefully, having strong friendships, looking after health, making space to grow spiritually, giving priority to growing congregational vision and community, developing leadership styles that both inspire and empower others, being aware of the pressures in small congregations, and developing a range of coping strategies.[26] These may sound prosaic and unspiritual in a discussion of God's love, but love is expressed in the details and love holds us to the best so that we honour our vows and commitments. Love for God requires that we know and love ourselves so that we can be ourselves in ministry and not constantly projecting an image that we can't live up to. We can only lay down our lives if we have first owned them.

Lest all this seem to be too serious, it is salutary to remind ourselves of Michael Ramsey's wisdom about keeping a sense of proportion in all things:

> Use your sense of humour. Laugh about things. Laugh at the absurdities of life. Laugh about yourself and about your own absurdity. . . . We are all of us infinitesimally small and ludicrous creatures within God's universe. You have to be serious, but never solemn, because if you are solemn about anything there is the risk of you becoming solemn about yourself.[27]

If we can communicate that to others, we will be fulfilling our diaconal vocation, since 'Joy is the infallible sign of the presence of God'[28] and we are called to make God's presence known.

> Many lives will be healed and made strong by your teaching, your care, your love for them. . . . In the coming years you will know the wound of Christ more than in the past, and you will also know the peace more than you know it now. And one day many will thank God for all that you will have done to make the wounds and the peace known to them.[29]

That is the outcome of love, God's transforming love.

9

Remember

Memory

Memory is central to biblical faith and life, evidenced by the consistent refrain that exhorts the people to remember what God has done in their history. It is not just memory that recalls, but memory that inhabits, so that our future draws on and is shaped by it. Years ago in a TV documentary about feminism, a woman interviewee observed, 'When you have a past, then you can have a future.' We take our example from the fact that God remembers (Exodus 2.24). Thus Deuteronomy 8 is full of exhortations to remember in life-changing ways, whilst Moses used song to exhort the people to remember (Deuteronomy 32.7). This is a reminder that song is a powerful aid to memory, hence the importance of well-chosen hymns that can build useful memory for the singers.[1] We need to look back if we are to understand how we reached the present, and thus how to move forward into the future. This is particularly true where we need to break free from a past cycle in order to move forward in new and more life-giving ways. That is true in counselling, and it is true in theological terms. And so the people were to look back to the rock from which they were hewn in order to have the capacity to envisage that the Lord would comfort Zion (Isaiah 51.1, 3).

That is a more theological way of putting Kierkegaard's observation that we live our lives forwards but understand them backwards. We could also say that it is another aspect of ministry on the margins, in this case the margins of the past and the future. Deacons are called in their catechetical ministry to stand on that threshold, to interpret the past so that people can build a future with God, perhaps thereby being freed from the tyranny of the present where that is oppressive.

Telling stories is central to developing memory and building faith. The Jewish people set an example in the telling and retelling of their salvation stories so that young children imbibe and inhabit them from infancy – the Passover story and Esther's story, told with dressing up at Hanukkah, being good examples. At a more mundane level, my father said he could never leave a word out of the *Thomas the Tank Engine* stories when my brother and I were little since we knew them by heart and complained when he wasn't reading by the book. Learning the stories is easy in childhood, and faith-building stories can be formative if they are modelled as such by adults in the faith community. Diaconal catechetical ministry is about helping children and adults to learn the stories of the faith and thus to build usable memory. It is also about helping them to bring personal memories to the liturgy for integration into the story of the community, thus giving them a wider context in the faith tradition.

Hope is memory. The community of faith has always been a community of hope because it is never left just with its own present resources. Over and again, in hopeless situations, the Old Testament writers evoked images out of the past that called forth trust that the future also belonged to God. The Brazilian theologian Rubem Alves reminds us that 'in the biblical world, one hopes for the future because one has already seen the creative event taking place in the past'.

Over and again the community of faith draws hope from its memory of God's work.[2]

Stories are powerful and we defuse them when we tell them just as moral fables with the 'lesson' pointed out. Catechesis is based on asking questions, and good stories ask us questions. We don't expect to be told what clues to look for as we read a crime novel, it is the experience of the story that makes it exciting and keeps us asking questions until we know who did it. Why then pre-empt the experience of the Christian story? Deacons preparing people for baptism are faced with a wealth of images and stories that can keep people asking questions, so long as we do not explain them away first. Thus in Salisbury Cathedral Chapter House, the stone carvings of Old Testament stories make good baptismal instruction and the bishop takes the candidates to look at them before baptizing them at the Easter dawn service, laying the foundation which the Vigil liturgy picks up a few minutes later in the dark outside the west front of the cathedral and continues to tell throughout the rest of the service. Then the candidates' experience can be put in dialogue with the tradition and questions asked afterwards. If we have explained everything in baptism preparation, what is left for the experience of baptism? The early bishops wisely saved much of their baptismal instruction until after the event; in the days after Easter they instructed the newly baptized so that their memories of dying and rising in the waters of baptism acquired meaning and became formative. There is a catechetical ministry among the newly baptized and deacons can build useful memory by being there after the event, helping people to ask and answer the questions their memories raise.

This raises questions for us – do we remember, have we made meaning from, our own stories? We can only help others to build usable memories if we have done so ourselves, if we have asked ourselves the sometimes intriguing, sometimes hard, questions in our own experience and have developed memories to build our faith. We cannot escape our history even if we try to deny it. To lose our sense of our history with God is to lose a vital resource for the future. Karl Marx wrote, 'It is out of our old history that new history must be made',[3] and in that Marxist context it is fascinating to see how the Museums of the Occupation in the Baltic States tell the history of the Nazi and Soviet periods, presenting information often visually and without comment but letting it ask the questions of the (predominantly young) visitors that will shape the way new history is made. We can learn from them and ponder how we tell the stories, what kind of memories we build, and what new history we will enable people to make with God.

This is equally true of much diaconal pastoral ministry at times of enormous and traumatic questions – Why did this happen? Can life go on in the face of this horror? Where is God now? Pastoral care in these circumstances is initially to sustain the person in need, not necessarily to answer the questions that are often asked rhetorically rather than with a desire for tidy answers. Many know the experience of trying to answer such questions, and realizing very quickly that the questioner does not want or cannot cope with the answer: the important thing at this stage is simply to tell the stories and ask the questions, again and again if necessary, and have it all heard.

Following the Cornish floods in 2004 the police asked clergy from the surrounding area to help. 'People need to tell and retell their stories; and then what's happened to them will begin to sink in. A lot of people have said how much they appreciated having someone who could just sit and listen, and offer support and a comforting hand, which is all we can do at the moment.'[4] But later the deacon can again come alongside those in distress and piece together the fragments so that some beginnings of answers can emerge when the person is ready. Then the painful memories can surface, ask their questions and be explored so that usable memory can soften the pain and pave the way for a future – in Walter Brueggemann's terms it is the pattern of orientation, disorientation and reorientation that is so clear in the Psalms.[5] The process takes time, and deacons will be there alongside, helping to build reserves of memory.

As deacons we should do this for ourselves not only with the stories of our lives but also with our history and memories of our ordination when we responded to the call to this ministry. If we cease to be aware of the nature and shape of our vocation, there is the danger of becoming unfocused or careless in our living out of our calling. Simon Patrick's advice to his clergy in Chichester in the seventeenth century is apposite today: 'Remember and read over frequently the vows that you made to God at your ordination, and the charge that was then given you, and examine yourselves frequently whether you do observe these or not.'[6] One way of doing this is to mark the anniversary of ordination with some reflection and thanksgiving as well as spiritual stock-taking, or to use Lent as a time of intentional self-examination. John Wesley was specific when he wrote to clergy, encouraging them to ask themselves:

And 1. What was my Intention in taking upon me this Office and Ministry? . . . Was it always, and is it now, wholly and solely, to glorify GOD, and save Souls? Has my Eye been singly fixed on this, from the Beginning hitherto? Had I never, have I not now, any Mixture in my Intention; and Alloy of baser Metal? Had I, or have I no Thought of worldly Gain. Filthy Lucre, as the Apostle terms it? Had I at first, have I now, no secular View? No Eye to Honour or Preferment? To Plentiful Income? Or, at least, a Competency? A Warm and comfortable Livelihood?[7]

This reflection is but part of the building of memory to undergird diaconal ministry; it begins long before ordination and continues in training. Study is an essential component of building memory and Michael Ramsey's wise encouragement is to '[t]hink of study as being refreshed from the deep, sparkling well of truth, which is Christ himself'. [8] My experience of training many people for ordination is that, whilst some approach their studies with apprehension, most soon become enthralled with the study of theology and find their understanding and awe of God is enlarged rather than their faith threatened. I think of a recent conversation with a student who could barely contain his excitement following study of God's Trinitarian love for the world and the shape that gives to the ministry of the Church. His exhilaration that this theological framework gave deeper meaning to all he had previously believed was contagious and exemplified Anselm's description of faith seeking understanding. We are caught up in that seeking understanding as we build memories when our faith is deepened and clarified through study, life experience and worship. Such memory building will bear fruit in our lives, enabling us to be the people and the example for which the Church prayed at our ordination:

Through your spirit, heavenly Father,
make these your servants faithful to serve
and constant in advancing your gospel in the world.
May they follow the example of Jesus Christ your Son,
who washed the feet of this disciples,
and set the needs of others before his own. [9]

When we know the pattern of God's ways, when that memory is part of us, then we can detect the patterns as they play out in new circumstances encountered in ministry. These memories and new experiences give us confidence to take godly risks. Thomas Merton wrote that 'when we understand the dialectic of life and death, we will learn to take risks implied by faith, to make the choices that deliver us from the routine self and open to us the door of a new being, a new reality'. [10] As deacons we first walk this way for ourselves so that when we go into the highways and byways of the world, when we stand on the margins of society, we know the path to walk alongside others. And we never finish the journey for ourselves: Euros Bowen's poem 'Leaves and Flowers and Fruit' points to the mystery of seasonal rhythms in our lives, of hope and memory, and the miracle that even hopelessness is not final but will bear fruit. Grafted into God's life, we will bear the fruit of God's wider ways with the world than our own little bit of it.

> When there are leaves and flowers and fruit
> on the same tree,
> the spring
> will make the summer sprout
> in the bush,
> and the summer will be a basket
> in autumn's grasp,
> like the past
> colouring the growth of the present,
> and the present giving fragrance
> to the juices that will be.
>
> Hope strikes its roots
> in the seasons of history.
> That is why it survives
> the winter weather,
> although that weather makes barren the boldness of the eye
> leaves time unprotected
> and snatches away all the memory's beliefs.
>
> Yet there are still leaves and flowers and fruit
> on the tree
> in the land of hopelessness,
> Ishmael
> under the bush
> in the wilderness,
> Moses
> in a basket
> in the midst of the bulrushes,
> Pryderi
> the hand that sets Rhiannon free.[11]

Imagination

We do not build our memory simply to be antiquarians or custodians of the past, although passing on the tradition is part of our vocation. Instead, we remember the past in order to be daring and creative in the present, and hopeful for the future. We who inherit a tradition, who know what God has done in the past, are called to lively ministry now. It was because Jesus was so rooted in the tradition of his people that some of his actions were so amazing to those around him who were faced with the need for imagination as they saw the enlargement and redefinition of the known, the pushing back of the boundaries. This is, in part, what caused offence to the religious leaders Jesus encountered, but what was happening to the disciples? We know that at times they struggled with this expansion of their world, but by Pentecost they were ready to imagine something new and to risk all for it. Their memories fuelled something gloriously new and life-giving as they just about kept up with the Spirit's presence and work in the world. It is always tempting to cling to security, to close our imagination down in the search for stability, but God calls us to let the memory of the past, however confusing, be the catalyst for faith and hope.

> They came, as dawn was breaking,
> to finalise their loss,
> absorb death's grim, stark meaning,
> the horror of the cross.
> They came, and angels told them,
> 'Recall the words he said.
> You seek the one now living,
> why look among the dead?'
>
> We dream of resurrection
> yet when it comes we cling
> to things known and familiar,
> the boundaries they bring.
> And we, who are not ready
> to let our grieving go,
> reject the angels' story,
> hold to the loss we know.

You interrupt our mourning,
an untrod path you pave;
for you bring resurrection
while we still seek the grave.
Our lives are wrenched wide open,
the wounds we nursed exposed;
and, like a phrase of music,
our death to life transposed.[12]

We can nurture hope for the future by letting our imagination
lead us into God's resurrection life that takes the melody of our
lives and transposes it into new keys. Our imaginations can lead us
in many directions and someone has said that the important thing
is that we learn to use our imagination in a way that will lead us
into the spaciousness of the gospel, letting us become the kind of
people whose hearts can be enlarged, the kind of people therefore
who can keep company with God whose heart knows no bounds.
If we use our imagination in a way that cramps us, the results may
look very proper but we shall end up with a world too small for
God.[13] Perhaps we can learn from Paul, writing to the Philippians,
when he charged them: 'Finally, beloved, whatever is true, whatever
is honourable, whatever is just, whatever is pure, whatever is pleas-
ing, whatever is commendable, if there is any excellence and if there
is anything worthy of praise, think about these things' (Philippians
4.8). This is not simply mind over matter, but it is recognition of
the formative power of memory and thought. Here William Temple
explains: 'Our characters are shaped by our companions and by the
objects to which we give most of our thoughts and with which we fill
our imaginations. We cannot always be thinking about Christ, but
we can refuse to dwell on any thoughts which are out of tune with
Him at any time when those thoughts come in.'[14] And thinking leads
to the practice of what we think about. Brother Lawrence's counsel
from his monastery kitchen is to put our memory of what is good
into practice, '[t]hat all things are possible to him who believes, that
they are less difficult to him who hopes, they are more easy to him
who loves, and still more easy to him who perseveres in the practice
of these three virtues'.[15]

The trouble with ministry is that there is frequently so much to keep in balance that we lose the ability to stand back and take time out, to look at things differently or creatively. There is always something else to do. Most of us begin ordained ministry with ideals to which we hope to hold ourselves – time to pray, time to relax, time with the family – and soon find that they slip down the list of priorities when other things cry more raucously for our attention. But if we are to be people of memory there has to be time to remember, if we are to be people with imagination there has to be time to dream with God. Perhaps we need to remember and take to heart the Genesis account of God resting on the seventh day, enjoying the very good creation. If God could rest, and we are created in God's image, we too can rest and the first step may be to give ourselves permission to do so. 'Our commitments of all kinds hold us so tightly, keep us so constrained, that we have little room for change. Sabbath is an invitation to imagine our lives differently. In risking Sabbath we discover that life can be lived without the control that reduces us and leaves us fatigued.'[16] A stock-taking question for all deacons could be, how do we nurture a godly imagination? And when is the Sabbath in our lives?

Hope

Diaconal ministry takes its example and its motivation from Jesus Christ. Therefore, death and resurrection lie at the heart of the diaconal vocation. In the death and resurrection of Christ we see the hallmark of God's pattern of working in the world. The author of the letter to the Hebrews exhorts us to consider Jesus so that we may not grow weary or lose heart (Hebrews 12.1–2), and thus to draw our own strength from his example. We will find ourselves as deacons in many situations where we have to recall the example of Christ and his steadfastness in order to endure the present circumstances, and to keep ourselves faithful and hopeful. Writing of work with those who have, for whatever reason, lost hope, William Lynch has some useful insights for those engaged in Christian ministry who face situations where hope is in short supply and godly creativity and imagination are needed:

> This great traditional meaning of hope as that which helps us transcend our endless forms of impossibility, or prison, of darkness,

is complemented by an equally classic understanding of the word imagination. For one of the permanent meanings of imagination has been that it is the gift that envisions what cannot yet be seen, the gift that constantly proposes to itself that the boundaries of the possible are wider than they seem. Imagination, if it is in prison and has tried every exit, does not panic or move into apathy but sits down and tries to envision another way out. It is always slow to admit that all the facts are in, that all the doors have been tried, and that it is defeated. It is not so much that it has vision as that it is able to wait, to wait for a moment of vision which is not yet there, for a door that is not yet locked. It is not overcome by the absoluteness of the present moment.[17]

'It is not so much that it has vision as that it is able to wait . . . it is not overcome by the absoluteness of the present moment.' That is not being unrealistic, it is bringing memory, imagination and hope to bear on the suffering of the world in the sure knowledge that God is faithful and good. It may not know the answers, but it is prepared to wait and hope in God, as the Psalmist did, 'for I shall again praise him' (Psalm 42.5). God has given us the gift of being able to hope, yet the world loses sight of that in the midst of the horrors and calamities, if not downright evils, of life today. Bishop John Taylor wrote: 'Nothing is more needed by humanity today, and by the church in particular, than the recovery of "beyondness" in the whole of life to revive the springs of wonder and adoration.'[18] Diaconal ministry that can keep hope alive, that is not overcome by the absoluteness of the present moment, is a powerful and subversive gift. If the incarnation, death, resurrection and ascension of Christ are about anything, they are about God not being overcome by the present moment in human history but revealing his glory in and through it, thus turning the world upside down.

The Church bears witness to this godly hope in the midst of despair. The deacon does not do this alone but, as a public and representative minister of the Church, may be called on to embody and articulate this hope to others. It is essential that deacons can build hope, immersed as we are in the midst of the hopelessness of so much of life with its ambiguities and paradoxes. Immersion in liturgy, in worship, will help to build our own hope and thus to nurture the 'infectious enthusiasm, itself a child of hope, that leaders need if others are to be persuaded to share the vision'.[19]

In theological terms, hope is the ability to live through Holy Saturday, to stay in that liminal time between death and resurrection, on the margin between the loss of old certainties and hopes and the rebirth of something with God that draws on the past but opens up new and undreamed-of horizons. In a footnote to his discussion of exile in the biblical story, Walter Brueggemann quotes George Steiner, writing as a Jew of the Christian story:

There is one particular day in Western history about which neither historical record nor myth nor Scripture make report. It is a Saturday. And it has become the longest of days. We know of that Good Friday which Christianity holds to have been that of the cross. But the non-Christian, the atheist, knows of it as well. That is to say that he knows of the injustice, of the interminable suffering, of the waste, of the brute enigma of ending. . . . We know also about Sunday. To the Christian, that day signifies an intimation, both assured and precarious, both evident and beyond comprehension, of resurrection, of a justice and a love that have conquered death. If we are non-Christian or non-believers, we know of that Sunday in precisely analogous terms. . . . The lineaments of that Sunday carry the name of hope (there is no word less deconstructable).

But ours is the long day's journey of the Saturday. Between suffering, aloneness, unutterable waste on the one hand and the dream of liberation of rebirth on the other. In the face of the torture of a child, of the death of love which is Friday, even the greatest art and poetry are almost helpless. In the Utopia of the Sunday, the aesthetic will, presumably, no longer have logic or necessity. The apprehensions and figurations ... which tell of pain and of hope, of the flesh which is said to taste of ash and of the spirit which is said to have the savour of fire, are always Sabbatarian. They have risen out of an immensity of waiting which is that of man. Without them, how could we be patient?[20]

Diaconal ministry that takes place in marginal places, on the boundaries of society and the boundaries of faith, is ministry that is familiar with Holy Saturday – paradoxically both God's day of rest and the day of struggle with hope for the first disciples. To be called to diaconal ministry is to be called to offer ourselves, with our strengths and our weaknesses, our hopes and our fears, to the God for whom Holy Saturday is not a mistake or a sign of absence. To this we bring our own imagination and creativity, our own gifts and graces, in the ministry of Christ who came to bring life.

We trust that you are fully determined, by the grace of God, to give yourself wholly to his service, that you may draw all his people into that new life which God has prepared for those who love him.[21]

Afterword

Diaconal ministry is incarnational, it reflects and draws its motivation from the work of God in Christ. The three locations for diaconal ministry – the church, the world and the margins – cover all the territory of God's creative and redemptive work: nowhere is alien to a deacon because nowhere is alien to God. However awful humans may have made parts of the world, the territory is still God's and, as God's agents and ambassadors, deacons minister with wisdom not naivety.

Although diaconal ministry is enveloped in the incarnation, Gerald O'Collins writes of the danger of pretending that we have ever mastered the truth of it. Instead we are perpetually caught up in the mystery of God's love. Thus, in phrases that bring together all the strands of diaconal ministry – catechetical, care and worship – he reminds us that all our questions and conclusions

> remain part of the triple homage owed to God: the homage of our intellect and its exploration of truth; that of faithful discipleship in the service of love, justice and the common good; and that of our worship in praise of the divine benevolence and glorious beauty. Faced with the 'frightening and fascinating' self-revelation of God in Jesus Christ, we approach this awesome mystery with our minds on stretch, our hands at work and our hearts at prayer.[1]

Why do we do all this? Because God has called us to live to the praise of his glory, to be expressions of God's love, to be a church in mission:

Rejoice in God, rejoice,
praise echo through this place,
as organ thunders, voices sing
God's glorious grace.
With grateful hearts
sing evermore;
the living God
O, come, adore!

God's rich excess of love
endures from age to age,
a sumptuous love whose strength transcends
our power to gauge.
Such boundless love
transforms the earth,
brings light and life
and joy to birth.

How can we know this love,
how can we offer praise
without the eloquence of God
the Son displays?
We cannot tell
all love can be,
but glimpse with joy
its mystery.

O God of love, we long
to comprehend your ways,
to read your word that reads our lives
with searching gaze.
Direct our steps
that we may run
your paths with joy
O risen Son.

Our words yield to the Word
Who knows our yearning hearts,
come, Spirit, vivify the truth

God's word impart.
then send us out
to preach, proclaim,
the wonders of
your glorious name.[2]

Amen.

Notes

Foreword

1 The Church of England, ACCM Working Party, *Deacons in the Church*. London: CIO, 1974.
2 The Church of England, Working Party of the House of Bishops, *For Such a Time as This*. London: Church House Publishing, 2001.
3 Austin Farrer, *A Celebration of Faith*. London: Hodder & Stoughton, 1970, pp. 109ff.
4 Diocese of Salisbury, *The Distinctive Diaconate*. Salisbury: Sarum College Press, 2003.

Introduction

1 The Church of England, *Mission Shaped Church*. London: Church House Publishing, 2004.
2 *Mission Shaped Church*, pp. 81–2.
3 The Diocese of Salisbury, *The Distinctive Diaconate*. Salisbury: Sarum College Press, 2003.
4 For example, the United Reformed Church's Church Related Community Workers are not ordained and focus solely on community development work, whilst deacons in the Orthodox Church have a primarily liturgical function.
5 The Church of England, Working Party of the House of Bishops, *For Such a Time as This*. London: Church House Publishing, 2001.
6 The Church of England, *Common Worship: Ordinal Report by the Liturgical Commission 2004 (GS 1535)* incorporating The Revision Committee's initial proposals for the revision of GS 1535.
7 William Shakespeare, *Hamlet*, Act 4, Scene 5.
8 Esther de Waal, *Seeking God*. London: Collins Fount Paperback, 1983, p. 105.
9 The Church of England, *Deacons in the Ministry of the Church*. London: Church House Publishing, 1988, Section 293, p. 95.

Chapter 1

1 Patrick Thompson, 'The Priest as Teacher of Prayer', in Hubert S. Box (ed.), *Priesthood, by Various Writers*. London: SPCK, 1937, p. 277.

2 James Barrie, *The Little Minister*. London: Cassell, 1892, p. 25.

3 Ronnie Aitchison, *The Ministry of a Deacon*. Peterborough: Epworth, 2003, p. 152.

4 Eugene Peterson, *Under the Unpredictable Plant*. Grand Rapids: William B. Eerdmans, 1992, pp. 23, 136.

5 Nelson Mandela. Quoted in Esther de Waal, *Lost in Wonder*. Norwich: Canterbury Press, 2003, p. 153.

6 Douglas Dales, *Glory: The Spiritual Theology of Michael Ramsey*. Norwich: Canterbury Press, 2003, p. 106, quoting Michael Ramsey, *The Gospel and the Catholic Church*, 1936, p. 45.

7 The Rt Revd Tom Ray, Bishop of North Michigan, speaking to the North American Association of Deacons (undated tape).

8 Diocese of Salisbury, *The Distinctive Diaconate*. Salisbury: Sarum College Press, 2003, pp. 33–4.

9 Antonia Lynn, 'Finding Images' in Christine Hall (ed.), *The Deacon's Ministry*. Leominster: Gracewing, 1991, p. 104.

10 For example, the Revd Roy Overthrow served for some years as Deacon to the Bishop of Salisbury.

11 I.e., the presbyter is not ordained deacon first, but is ordained directly to that ministry, and deacons do not normally seek later ordination as presbyters.

12 Aitchison, *The Ministry of a Deacon*, p. 161.

13 The Revd Anthony Barratt, at a consultation on 'What Is Ordination?', Exeter, 2003.

14 Luke 22.27; see also Luke 12.37.

15 *The Rule of Benedict*, Chapter 2, in Joan Chittister, *The Rule of Benedict: Insights for the Ages*. New York: Crossroad, 1992.

16 *The Rule of Benedict*, Chapter 31.

17 *Evagrius Ponticus. The Praktikos*, ed. M. Basil Pennington. Spencer, MA: Cistercian Publications, 1970, p. 41.

18 The Church of England, *Common Worship: Ordinal Report by the Liturgical Commission 2004 (GS 1535)* incorporating The Revision Committee's initial proposals for the revision of GS 1535.

19 The Church of England, *The Alternative Service Book (1980)*, The Ordination of Deacons.

20 John Collins, *Diakonia: Reinterpreting the Ancient Sources*. Oxford: Oxford University Press, 1990; and *Deacons and the Church*. Leominster: Gracewing, 2002.

21 This is reflected in the ministry of and title given to 'Church Related Community Workers' in the United Reformed Church.

22 Ignatius, *Epistle to the Trallians*, 3.1. Similarly, in the *Epistle to the Magnesians*, 6, he says: 'Let the bishop preside in God's place, and the presbyters take the place of the apostolic council, and let the deacons (my special favourites) be entrusted with the ministry of Jesus Christ who was with the father from eternity and appeared at the end [of the world].'

23 Deidre Good, *Jesus the Meek King*. Harrisburg: Trinity Press International, 1999.

24 Drawn from The Church of England, Working Party of the House of Bishops, *For Such a Time as This*. London: Church House Publishing, 2001.

25 The Church of England, *Deacons in the Ministry of the Church*, London: Church House Publishing, 1988, p. 92.

26 Richard Hooker, *Of the Laws of Ecclesiastical Polity*, Books 1–5. Cambridge, MA: Harvard University Press, 1977, V.xxiv.1.

27 Sean Connolly, *Simple Priesthood*. London: St Paul's, 2001, p. 38.

28 Stephen F. B. Bedale, *The Training of a Priest*, in Box (ed.) *Priesthood, by Various Writers*, pp. 138–9.

29 Hooker, *Laws of Ecclesiastical Polity*, Book V. lxxvii.

30 Philip Sheldrake, *Spaces for the Sacred*. London: SCM Press, 2001, p. 84.

Chapter 2

1 Jarrett Kerr, 'Scott Holland: Drains and the Incarnation', *The Times*, 5 February 1983. Quoted in Christopher Gower, *Speaking of Healing*. London: SPCK, 2003, p. 17.

2 H. Maynard Smith, *Frank, Bishop of Zanzibar*. London: SPCK, 1926, p. 302.

3 Kathleen Norris, *Dakota: A Spiritual Geography*. Boston, New York: Houghton Mifflin, 1993, p. 164.

4 George Herbert, *The Country Parson*, Chapter 4, in *The Complete English Poems and The Country Parson*, ed. J. Tobin. London: Penguin, 1991.

5 Alasdair Macintyre, quoted in Kenneth Leech, *The Sky Is Red*. London: DLT, 1997, p. 207.

6 Rowan Williams, sermon in Canterbury Cathedral, 27 February 2003.

7 John Donne, *Devotions Upon Emergent Occasions*, XVII Meditation, in *Selections from Divine Poems, Sermons, Devotions and Prayers*, ed. John Booty. New York: Paulist Press, 1990.

8 David Say, 'Nudging the Government: Runcie and Public Affairs' in Stephen Platten (ed.), *Runcie: On Reflection*. Norwich: Canterbury Press, 2002, p. 33.

9 Gustavo Gutiérrez, *We Drink from Our Own Wells*. Maryknoll: Orbis, 1984, p. 112.

10 Leech, *The Sky Is Red*, pp. 140–1.

11 William Law, *A Serious Call to a Devout and Holy Life*. J. M. Dent & Co., 1906, p. 7.

12 Norris, *Dakota*, pp. 2–3.

13 Padraig Daly, 'Presence', in *The Last Dreamers*. Dublin: Dedalus, 1999, p. 125. Used with permission.

14 Norris, *Dakota*, pp. 74, 76.

15 Ben Quash, 'The Anglican Church as a Polity of Presence', in D. Dormor, J. McDonald and J. Caddick (eds), *Anglicanism: The Answer to Modernity*. London: Continuum, 2003, p. 49.

16 R. S. Thomas, 'Look', originally published in *Not That He Brought Flowers*. London: Hart-Davies, 1968.

17 R. S. Thomas, 'The Word', in *Collected Poems*, 1945–1990. London: J. M. Dent, a division of Orion Publishing, 1993. Used with permission.

18 Dietrich Bonhoeffer, *Letters and Papers from Prison*. London: SCM Press, 1953, 2001, p. 137.

19 'Spring', Gerard Manley Hopkins, in *Poems and Prose*. London: Penguin Classics, 1985.

20 Hopkins, *Poems and Prose*, pp. 106, 121.

21 Graham Dowell, *Enjoying the World: The Rediscovery of Thomas Traherne*. Harrisburg: Morehouse Publishing, 1990, p. 68.

22 Esther de Waal, *Seeking God*. London: Collins Fount Paperback, 1983, pp. 107, 108.

23 At a conference in Michigan in 1991.

Chapter 3

1 Michael Downey, *Worship at the Margins: Spirituality and Liturgy*. Washington: Pastoral Press, 1994, p. 75.

2 Philip Sheldrake, *Spaces for the Sacred*. London: SCM Press, 2001, pp. 30–1.

3 Diocese of Salisbury, *The Distinctive Diaconate*. Salisbury: Sarum College Press, 2003, p. 112.

4 Brooke Foss Westcott, *Some Aspects of Christianity*, 1887, pp. 72, 74, 75. Quoted in Graham Patrick, *Brooke Foss Westcott: The Miner's Bishop*. Peterborough: Epworth Press, 2004, p. 220.

5 John Chrysostom, *Homily XX*, in *St Chrysostom's Homilies on the Epistles of Paul to the Corinthians*, ed. Philip Schaff.

6 Monica Attias, 'Reconciliation and the Eucharist', in David Conway (ed.), *Living the Eucharist*. London: DLT, 2001, pp. 19, 20.

7 John Holdsworth, *Dwellers in a Strange Land*. Norwich: Canterbury Press, 2003, pp. 109–10.

8 Belden C. Lane, *The Solace of Fierce Landscapes*. Oxford: Oxford University Press, 1998, pp. 162–3.

9 Rowan Williams, *Silence and Honey Cakes*. London: Lion, 2003, p. 38.

10 Quoted in Williams, *Silence and Honey Cakes*, p. 25.

11 Benedicta Ward SLG (trans.), *Sayings of the Desert Fathers*. Oxford: A. R. Mowbray, 1981, p. 194.

12 Downey, *Worship at the Margins*, p. 82.

13 Dan Hardy, *Finding the Church: The Dynamic Truth of Anglicanism*. London: SCM Press, 2001, pp. 148–9.

14 James Dreounian, 'Reaping Benefit for Local Communities', *Planning*, 8 August 2003.

15 'The Porch', R. S. Thomas, in *Collected Poems 1945–1990*. London: J. M. Dent, a division of Orion Publishing. Used with permission.

16 Michael Mayne, *Pray, Love, Remember*. London: DLT, 1998, p. 83.

17 Mayne, *Pray, Love, Remember*, p. 8.

18 Melvyn Bragg, *A Son of War*. London: Hodder and Stoughton, 2001, pp. 64, 65.

19 *The Rule of Benedict*, Chapter 66, in Joan Chittister, *The Rule of Benedict. Insights for the Ages*. New York: Crossroad, 1992.

20 Chittister, *The Rule of Benedict*, p. 170.

21 Copyright © Rosalind Brown 1995.

22 Kathleen Norris, *Dakota: A Spiritual Geography*. Boston, New York: Houghton Mifflin, 1993, p. 63.

Chapter 4

1 Michael Ramsey, *Canterbury Essays and Addresses*. London: SPCK, 1964, p. 22.

2 Michael Ramsey, *The Gospel and the Catholic Church*. London: Longmans Green & Co., 1956, pp. 148–9.

3 A. C. Lichtenberger, 'The Social Implications of the Liturgical Renewal', in Massey Shepherd (ed.), *The Liturgical Renewal of the Church*. New York: Oxford University Press, 1960, pp. 101–20.

4 Massey Shepherd, *The Living Liturgy*. New York: Oxford University Press, 1946, pp. 7–8.

5 A question asked by Kathleen Ben Rabha, a Social Responsibility Officer for the Diocese of Salisbury.

6 Alan Webster in *The Times*, 10 April 2004.

7 Kenneth Leech, *Struggle in Babylon*. London: SPCK, 1988, pp. 185–6.

8 *The Rule of Benedict*, Chapter 20, in Joan Chittister, *The Rule of Benedict: Insights for the Ages*. New York: Crossroad, 1992.

9 *The Rule of Benedict*, Chapter 38.

10 Kennneth Leech, *The Sky Is Red*. London: DLT, 1997, p. 182, quoting Gail Ramshaw in Michael W. Merriman (ed.), *The Baptismal Mystery and the Catechumenate*. San Francisco: National Liturgical Conference, 1983, p. 73.

11 Richard Hooker, *Of the Laws of Ecclesiastical Polity*, Books 1–5. Cambridge, MA: Harvard University Press, 1977, V Chapter xxv.

12 Simon Patrick, *The Work of the Ministry, represented to the Clergy of the Diocese of Ely* (1692), in John R. H. Moorman (ed.), *The Curate of Souls: Being a Collection of Writings on the Nature and Work of a Priest from the First Century after the Restoration 1660–1760*. London: SPCK, 1958, p. 65.

13 David Stancliffe, 'The Fraction and the Shape of the Rite', in David Conway (ed.), *Living the Eucharist*. London: DLT, 2001 p. 98.

14 Michael Ramsey, *Be Still and Know*. London: Collins, 1982, pp. 13–14.

15 Izaac Walton, *Life of Mr George Herbert*, in *The Complete English Poems*. London: Penguin, 1991, pp. 300–1.

16 Belden C. Lane, *The Solace of Fierce Landscapes*. Oxford: Oxford University Press, 1998, p. 226.

17 Leech, *Struggle in Babylon*, p. 188.

18 *Common Worship: Service and Prayers for the Church of England*. London: Church House Publishing, 2000, p. 158.

19 Mother Mary Clare, *Encountering the Depths*. London: DLT, 1981, pp. 55, 50.

20 Quoted in David Wood, *Poet, Priest and Prophet: Bishop John V. Taylor*. London: CBTI, 2002, pp. 201–2.

21 Quoted in Ramsey, *The Gospel and the Catholic Church*, pp. 145–6.

22 Myra Blyth at STETS Easter School, 2000.

23 Aidan Kavanagh, *Elements of Rite: A Handbook of Liturgical Style*. New York: Pueblo, 1982, pp. 76–7.

24 See The Diocese of Salisbury, *The Distinctive Diaconate*. Salisbury: Sarum College Press, 2003, pp. 68–70, for a discussion of the question of whether deacons baptize.

Chapter 5

1 Eugene Peterson, *The Contemplative Pastor*. Grand Rapids: Wm B. Eerdmans Publishing Co., 1993, p. 15.

2 The Church of England, *Common Worship: Ordinal Report by the Liturgical Commission 2004 (GS 1535)* incorporating The Revision Committee's initial proposals for the revision of GS 1535.

3 John Henry Newman, quoted in E. Schillebeeckx, *God and Man*. London: Sheed and Ward, 1969/1979, p. 219.

4 W. H. Vanstone, 'A Pattern of Pastoral Ministry', in John Greenhalgh and Elizabeth Russell (eds), *Building in Love: The Vocation of the Church*. London: St Mary's Bourne Street, 1990, pp. 35–6.

5 Timothy Biles, *Church Wardens I Have Buried: The Journal of a Country Vicar 1998–99*. Bridport: Creeds, 2000, pp. 127–8.

6 David Stancliffe, *God's Pattern*. London: SPCK, 2003, p. 130.

7 Ben Quash, 'The Anglican Church as a Polity of Presence', in D. Dormor, J. McDonald and J. Caddick (eds), *Anglicanism: The Answer to Modernity*. London: Continuum, 2003, pp. 47–8.

8 Michael Ramsey, *The Christian Priest Today*. London: SPCK, 1956, p. 7.

9 Ronnie Aitchison, *The Ministry of a Deacon*. Peterborough: Epworth, 2003, p. 162.

10 Douglas Dales, *Glory: The Spiritual Theology of Michael Ramsey*. Norwich: Canterbury Press, 2003, p. 35.

11 Henri Nouwen, *The Way of the Heart*. London: DLT, 1981, p. 34.

12 In a talk given at Yale Divinity School in 1995. See also his several books.

13 Quoted in Kathryn Spink, *A Chain of Love*. London: SPCK, 1984, p. 113.

14 Quoted in Quash, 'The Anglican Church as Polity of Presence', pp. 46–7.

15 Eugene Peterson, *Under the Unpredictable Plant*. Grand Rapids: Wm B. Eerdmans, 1992, p. 139.

16 Michael Ramsey, *Durham Essays and Addresses*. London: SPCK, 1956, pp. 128–9.

17 Padraig Daly, 'Ministers' in *The Last Dreamers*. Dublin: Dedalus, 1999. Used with permission.

18 Michel Quoist, *Prayers of Life*. Dublin: Gill and Macmillan Ltd, 1963.

19 Gerard Manley Hopkins, Sermon for Sunday Evening 23rd November 1879 at Bedford Leigh, in *Poems and Prose*. London: Penguin Classics, 1985, p. 141.

20 Hopkins, From Note-Books, Journal etc., 23 July 1874, in *Poems and Prose*, p. 131.

21 Dietrich Bonhoeffer, *Letters and Papers from Prison*. London: SCM Press, 1953, 2001, p. 146.

22 Desmond Tutu, 'Running the Gauntlet: Runcie and South Africa', in Stephen Platten (ed.), *Runcie: On Reflection: an Archbishop Remembered*. Norwich: Canterbury Press, 2002, pp. 61–2.

23 Izaak Walton, *Life of Herbert*, in *The Complete Poems*. London: Penguin, 1991, p. 293.

24 Sean Connolly, *Simple Priesthood*. London: St Paul's, 2001, pp. 73–4.

25 The Monastic Community of Jesus, *In the Heart of the City, In the Heart of God*. Livre de Vie 41 and 44. Paris, 1997.

26 Richard Harries, 'Pastoral Pragmatist: Runcie as Communicator', in Stephen Platten (ed.), *Runcie: On Reflection*. Norwich: Canterbury Press, 2002, pp. 113–14.

27 William Lynch, *Images of Hope: Imagination as Healer of the Hopeless*. Notre Dame: University of Notre Dame Press, 1965, 1974, pp. 139, 179.

28 Copyright © Rosalind Brown 1995, Celebration. Theme hymn for the National Episcopal AIDS Coalition conference, 'Hope and Healing', St Louis, MO, September 1995. Tune: Sussex.

29 David Lyall, *The Integrity of Pastoral Care*. London: SPCK, 2001, p. 74.

30 Francis de Sales, *On the Love of God*. Methuen and Co. 1902, p. 94.

31 Mother Mary Clare, *Encountering the Depths*. London: DLT, 1981, pp. 47–8.

32 The Methodist Church, *What Is a Deacon?* Report to the Methodist Conference, 2004, 5.10 and 5.12.

33 Copyright © Rosalind Brown, 1995 Celebration. Tune: Kingsfold.

Chapter 6

1 Gerald O'Collins, *Incarnation*. London, New York: Continuum, 2002, p. vii.

2 The Church of England, *Common Worship: Ordinal Report by the Liturgical Commission 2004 (GS 1535)* incorporating the Revision Committee's initial proposals for the revision of GS 1535.

3 The Methodist Church, *What Is a Deacon?* Report to the Methodist Conference, 2004, 5.1 and 5.4.

4 George Herbert, *The Country Parson*, Chapter 21, in *The Complete English Poems and The Country Parson*, ed. J. Tobin. London: Penguin, 1991.

5 Herbert, *The Country Parson*, Chapter 21.

6 Jeremy Taylor, *Rules and Advices to the Clergy of the Diocese of Down and Connor; For their deportment in the Personal and Publick Capacities*. 1661, Ch. 1, in John R. H. Moorman (ed.), *The Curate of Souls: Being a Collection of Writings on the Nature and Work of a Priest from the First Century after the Restoration 1660–1760*. London: SPCK, 1958.

7 Henry Dodwell, *Two Letters of Advice; For the Susception of Holy Orders*, 1672, XXII and XXIII, in Moorman (ed.), *The Curate of Souls*, p. 69.

8 Simon Patrick, *The Work of the Ministry, represented to the Clergy of the Diocese of Ely*, 1692, in Moorman (ed.), *The Curate of Souls*.

9 Michel Quoist, *With Open Heart*. Dublin: Gill and Macmillan, 1983, p. 50.

10 Anonymous, *Advice to a young Clergyman how to Conduct Himself in the Common Offices of Life* (1730), in Moorman (ed.), *The Curate of Souls*, p. 176.

11 The Church of England, *For Such a Time as This*. London: Church House Publishing, 2001, Chapter 7.

12 Julian of Norwich, *Revelations of Divine Love*. London: Penguin, 1966, p. 130.

13 John Stobbart, *The Wisdom of Evelyn Underhill*. Mowbray, 1951, p. 11.

14 William Abraham, *The Logic of Evangelism*. Grand Rapids: William B. Eerdmans Publishing Co., 1989.

15 Mother Mary Clare, *Encountering the Depths*. London: DLT, 1981, p. 62.

16 Walter Brueggemann, *Finally Comes the Poet*. Minneapolis: Augsburg, Fortress Press, 1989, p. 29.

17 The Rt Revd Tom Ray, Bishop of North Michigan, speaking to the North American Association of Deacons (undated tape).

18 John Inge, *A Christian Theology of Place*. Aldershot: Ashgate, 2003, p. 124.

19 D. Kemmis, *Community and the Politics of Place*. Norman, OK: University of Oklahoma Press, 1990, pp. 79, 138, quoted in Inge, *A Christian Theology of Place*, p. 131.

Chapter 7

1 Michael Ramsey, *The Christian Priest Today*. London: SPCK, 1972, p. 15.

2 The Church of England, *Common Worship: Ordinal Report by the Liturgical Commission 2004 (GS 1535)* incorporating The Revision Committee's initial proposals for the revision of GS 1535.

3 K. K. Fitzgerald, *Women Deacons in the Orthodox Church: Called to Holiness and Ministry*, quoted in Ninni Smedberg, 'The Quest for a Spirituality for the Deacon', in G. Borgegard, O. Fanuelsen and C. Hall, *The Ministry of the Deacon 2. Ecclesiological Explorations*. Uppsala: Nordic Ecumenical Council, undated, p. 147.

4 Colin Buckland and John Earwicker, *Leaders Under Pressure*. Crusade for World Revival, 1996. See Christopher Cocksworth and Rosalind Brown, *Being a Priest Today*. Norwich: Canterbury Press, 2002, p. 103 and Chapter 6 footnote 2.

5 Canon C26 states, 'Every bishop, priest or deacon is under obligation, not being let by sickness or some other urgent cause, to say daily the

Morning and Evening Prayer, either privately or openly.' See Cocksworth and Brown, *Being a Priest Today*, Chapter 6.

6 Forbes Robinson, *Letters to His Friends*. London: Spottiswoode and Co., 1904, p. 165.

7 Michael Mayne, *Pray, Love, Remember*. London: DLT, 1998, p. 24.

8 Hugh Montefiore, *Sermons from Great St Mary's*. William Collins Sons and Co., 1968, p. 16.

9 See also the chapter on 'Being for Prayer' in Cocksworth and Brown, *Being a Priest Today*.

10 Mother Teresa, in Kathryn Spink, *In the Silence of the Heart*. London: SPCK, 1983, p. 17.

11 Baron Frederick von Hugel, *Letters to a Niece*. J. M. Dent and Sons, 1929, p. 123.

12 Brother Lawrence, *The Practice of the Presence of God*. Mowbray and Co., 1977, p. 19.

13 Jeremy Taylor, source untraced. Quoted in Mayne, *Pray, Love, Remember*, p. 22.

14 Douglas Dales, *Glory: The Spiritual Theology of Michael Ramsey*. Norwich: Canterbury Press, 2003, p. 135.

15 John Udris, 'Conversion: The Call within a Calling', in Sean Connolly, *Simple Priesthood*. London: St Paul's, 2001, pp. 36, 143.

16 Joan Chittister, *The Rule of Benedict: Insights for the Ages*. New York: Crossroad, 1992, pp. 116–17.

17 Michael Ramsey, *Jesus and the Living Past*, quoted in Dales, *Glory*, p. 37.

18 Connolly, *Simple Priesthood*, pp. 53–4.

19 Connolly, *Simple Priesthood*. p. 55.

20 Gregory's letter to Eulogius, Archbishop of Alexandria, AD 598, quoted in Dales, *Glory*, p. 43.

21 Jeremy Taylor, *Rules and Advices to the Clergy of the Diocese of Down and Connor; For their deportment in the Personal and Publick Capacities*, 1661, S15, in John R. H. Moorman (ed.), *The Curate of Souls: Being a Collection of Writings on the Nature and Work of a Priest from the First Century after the Restoration 1660–1760*. London: SPCK, 1958, p. 8.

22 Belden C. Lane, *The Solace of Fierce Landscapes*. Oxford: Oxford University Press, 1998, p. 173.

23 Thomas Merton, *Contemplative Prayer*. London: DLT, 1973, p. 144.

24 Kenneth Leech, *The Sky Is Red*. London: DLT, 1997, p. 31.

25 Kenneth Leech, *True Prayer*. London: DLT, 1981, p. 13.

Chapter 8

1 Gerard Manley Hopkins, 'Let me be to Thee', Four early poems 1865–66, in *Poems and Prose*. London: Penguin Classics, 1985.

2 Thomas Traherne, *The Centuries*, The Second Century, 65, in *Thomas Traherne Selected Poems and Prose*, ed. A. Bradford. London: Penguin, 1991.

3 Kenneth Leech, *The Sky Is Red*. London: DLT, 1997, p. 122.

4 Quoted in David Wood, *Poet, Priest and Prophet: Bishop John V. Taylor*. London: CBTI, 2002, p. 202.

5 John Wesley, *An Address to the Clergy*, 1756, in John R. H. Moorman (ed.), *The Curate of Souls: Being a Collection of Writings on the Nature and Work of a Priest from the First Century after the Restoration 1660–1760*. London: SPCK, 1958, p. 218.

6 Basil Hume, *To Be a Pilgrim*. Slough: St Paul Publications, 1984.

7 The Ordination of Deacons in the Church of Sweden.

8 Stanley Kunitz (ed.), *The Essential Blake*. New York: Ecco Press, 1987, p. 91.

9 Hans Küng, *On Being a Christian*. William Collins Sons and Co., 1977, p. 256.

10 The Church of England, *Criteria for Selection*. ABM Paper 3b, 1993, Criterion F.

11 Simon Patrick, *The Work of the Ministry, represented to the Clergy of the Diocese of Ely*, 1692, in John R. H. Moorman (ed.), *The Curate of Souls: Being a Collection of Writings on the Nature and Work of a Priest from the First Century after the Restoration 1660–1760*. London: SPCK, 1958, pp. 76–7.

12 Henry Dodwell, *Two Letters of Advice; For the Susception of Holy Orders*, 1672, XXIV, in Moorman, *The Curate of Souls*, pp. 47–8.

13 For an introduction to Symeon's writings on our relationship to the material creation, see Anestis G. Keselopoulos, *Man and the Environment*. Crestwood, NY: St Vladimir's Seminary Press, 2001.

14 R. S. Thomas, 'Look', in *Not that He Brought Flowers*. London: Hart-Davis, 1968.

15 Copyright © Rosalind Brown 2001. Tune: Ton-y-Botel / Ebeneezer.

16 The Church of England, *Common Worship: Ordinal Report by the Liturgical Commission 2004 (GS 1535)* incorporating The Revision Committee's initial proposals for the revision of GS 1535.

17 John 13.1–17.

18 Sven Erik Brodd, 'Caritas and Diakonia as Perspectives on the Diaconate', in G. Borgegard and C. Hall (eds), *The Ministry of the Deacon Volume 2: Ecclesiological Explorations*. Uppsala: Nordic Ecumenical Council, 2000, p. 36.

19 Patrick, *The Work of the Ministry*, in Moorman, *The Curate of Souls*.

20 Sean Connolly, *Simple Priesthood*. London: St Paul's, 2001, p. 74.

21 W. H. Vanstone in the hymn, 'Morning glory, star lit sky'.

22 W. H. Vanstone, 'A Pattern of Pastoral Ministry', in John Greenhalgh and Elizabeth Russell (eds), *Building in Love: The Vocation of the Church*. London: St Mary's Bourne Street, 1990, p. 36.

23 Belden C. Lane, *The Solace of Fierce Landscapes*, pp. 90, 91, 94–5.

24 Frederick Beechner, published source not known.

25 George Herbert, 'Love (3)', in *The Complete English Poems and The Country Parson*, ed. J. Tobin. London: Penguin, 1991.

26 Peter Kaldor and Rod Bulpitt, *Burnout*. Adelaide: Openbook Publishers. Cited in *Quadrant*, March 2004.

27 Michael Ramsey, quoted in Margaret Duggan, *Through the Year with Michael Ramsey*. London: Hodder and Stoughton, 1975, p. 81.

28 Leon Bloy. Source unknown.

29 Michael Ramsey, *The Christian Priest Today*. London: SPCK, 1972, p. 87.

Chapter 9

1 See Rosalind Brown, *How Hymns Shape Our Lives*. Cambridge: Grove, 2001.

2 Bruce C. Birch, 'By the Waters of Babylon', *Sojourners*, October 1984, p. 28.

3 Karl Marx, quoted in Kenneth Leech, *The Sky Is Red*. London: DLT, 1997, p. 1.

4 The Revd Christine Musser in *Church Times*, 20 August 2004.

5 Walter Brueggemann, *The Psalms and the Life of Faith*. Minneapolis: Fortress Press, 1995, pp. 9–15, and *The Message of the Psalms: A Theological Commentary*. Minneapolis: Augsburg, 1984.

6 Simon Patrick, *A Letter of the Bishop of Chichester to his Clergy*, 1690, in John R. H. Moorman, *The Curate of Souls: Being a Collection of Writings on the Nature and Work of a Priest from the First Century after the Restoration 1660–1760*. London: SPCK, 1958, p. 51.

7 John Wesley, *A Letter of Advice to Clergy*, 1756, in Moorman, *The Curate of Souls*, p. 228.

8 Source not traced.

9 The Church of England, *Common Worship: Ordinal Report by the Liturgical Commission 2005 (GS 1535)* incorporating The Revision Committee's initial proposals for the revision of GS 1535.

10 Thomas Merton, *New Seeds of Contemplation*. Burns and Oates, 1962, p. 13.

11 Euros Bowen, 'Leaves and Flowers and Fruit', in *Euros Bowen: Priest-poet*. Penarth: Church in Wales Publications, 1993.

12 Copyright © Rosalind Brown 1995. Possible tune: Thornbury.

13 Source untraced.

14 William Temple, *Christian Faith and Life*. London: SCM Press, 1963, p. 43.

15 Brother Lawrence, *The Practice of the Presence of God*. Mowbray and Co., 1977, p. 19.

16 Walter Brueggemann, *Finally Comes the Poet*. Minneapolis: Augsburg Fortress Press, 1989, p. 97.

17 William Lynch, *Images of Hope: Imagination as Healer of the Hopeless*. Notre Dame: University of Notre Dame Press, 1965, 1974, p. 35.

18 John V. Taylor, *The Go-Between God*. London: SCM Press, 1973, p. 45.

19 John Perry, *Christian Leadership*. Sevenoaks: Hodder and Stoughton, 1983, p. 86.

20 George Steiner, *Real Presences: Is There Anything in What We Say?*, quoted in Walter Brueggemann, *Theology of the Old Testament*. Minneapolis: Fortress Press, 1997, p. 201 footnote 42.

21 The Church of England, *Common Worship: Ordinal Report by the Liturgical Commission 2004 (GS 1535)* incorporating The Revision Committee's initial proposals for the revision of GS 1535.

Afterword

1 Gerald O'Collins, *Incarnation*. London, New York: Continuum, 2002, p. vii.

2 Copyright © Rosalind Brown 2002. Tune: Darwall's 148th.